The Riven Oak
and the
Ivy
or
The Maid of Saragoza

*A Romance of the
War for Southern Independence*

Ye who shall marvel when you hear her tale,
Oh! had you known her in her softer hour,
Mark'd her black eye that mocks her coal-black veil,
Heard her light, lively tones in Lady's bower,
Seen her long locks that foil the painter's power,
Her fairy form, with more than female grace,
Scarce would you deem that Saragoza's tower
Beheld her smile in Danger's Gorgon face,
Thin the closed ranks and lead in Glory's fearful chase.
— Childe Harold, *Canto I*, Stanza 55

Major Thomas Preston

The
Scuppernong Press
Wake Forest, NC
www.scuppernongpress.com

The Riven Oak and the Ivy
or
The Maid of Saragoza
A Romance of the War for Southern Independence

By Major Thomas Preston

©2023 The Scuppernong Press

First Printing

The Scuppernong Press
PO Box 1724
Wake Forest, NC 27588
www.scuppernongpress.com

Cover artwork by Elizabeth Preston
Book design by Frank B. Powell, III

All rights reserved

Printed in the United States of America

No part of this book may be reproduced or transmitted in any form or by any means, electronic or mechanical, including photocopying, recording, or by any information and storage and retrieval system, without written permission from the editor and/or publisher.

International Standard Book Number ISBN 978-1-942806-57-8

Library of Congress Control Number: 2023947904

They Were The Knightliest Of The Knightly Race
Who Since The Days Of Old,
Have Kept The Lamp Of Chivalry
Alight In Hearts Of Gold.
— Confederate Monument At Corinth

Introduction

The subject of the War Between the States, as it pertained to Jackson County, Texas, and the story of the Confederacy, and its quest for independence, was one which provided ample grist from which a romance writer might glean the bountiful harvest of an inspired story. The conflict itself was not over emancipation of the slaves, though that event was a result of the war, but over different systems of economy: one commercial and industrial, the other largely agricultural. America had become two peoples, one seeking dominion over all peoples and all things, the other contented with the blessings bestowed by the good earth. Though the two peoples were joined by a written constitution, a numerical majority of one section imposed protective tariffs on the imports of the other. Tariffs are a bounty to one, a burden to the other. Tariffs have the effect of levying an unequal, and therefore unconstitutional, tax on the consumer.

Thus, it will be seen that every former Confederate repudiates all accusations of fighting to preserve the institution of slavery. The effort of the enemy to destroy it without compensation was practical robbery, which, of course, the South resisted. The refusal of Lincoln's suggested compensation at Fortress Monroe, after the destruction had already occurred, clearly shows the Confederate struggle to have been for the right of self-government, which the Englishman has claimed, and fought for, since the days of King John.

This narrative, then, has as a backdrop, the struggle of the people of the South to resist the Yankee leviathan. The fledgling nation, disadvantaged in both manpower and materiel, held the enemy at bay. The South, after mustering every able-bodied man, could enroll, in all, but 600,000 soldiers, while she fought 2,600,000. Never was there a war continued for four years at such fearful odds. And yet Richmond, the Confederate capital, almost in sight of Washington, was only captured when Sherman and Sheridan, the modern Attila's, had flanked it with walls of fire, and pillaged the country in its rear. Never has there been a war in which the weaker so long and so effectually held the stronger at bay or so often defeated them on the field of battle; never a war in which the valor of the vanquished was so respected by foes and so universally applauded by the world.

The Confederate Army in the West, denominated the Army of Tennessee, was composed of brave and determined soldiers who had an unshakable belief in the destiny of the Southern people to become free and independent.

But besides the legal argument of the right of secession, it was a just war in defense of hearth and home. In Tennessee, Mississippi and Louisiana there were many examples of Northern pillaging and senseless destruction. These ravages lay considerable hardship upon the Southern people, who responded with a determination to see this war to its absolute end.

The author confesses an inability to do justice to the character, services, and devotion of the women of the Confederacy. They gave to the armies their husbands, fathers, sons, and brothers, with aching hearts, and bade them good-bye with sobs and tears. But they believed their sacrifice was due to their country and her cause. They assumed the care of their homes and of the children and the aged. Many of them, having been raised in luxury, had to engage now in all the hundred menial tasks and drudgery of the farm and shop. Even field work was now required of them to furnish the means to feed their families. Spinning wheels and looms were produced where none had been seen before, forever sending to the soldiers in the field something to wear or eat. Like ministering angels, they visited and attended the hospitals, with lint and bandages for the wounded, with medicine for the sick, and such nourishment as they could obtain.

In this narrative you will find a vivid picture of the female strongly animated against the invader. They beat their male relatives hollow in their denunciations and hopes of vengeance. The fortitude of the Southern woman on the home front has everything to do with keeping their husbands, sons, and brothers in the field. The Southern lady is no wallflower, and her vocal pluck recalls the Spartan mother who admonishes her soldier to return home, either with his shield, or upon it.

It is the story of the O'Berry mother who lost four sons in battle, (all of whom were in Company "K" of the Second Texas), and who is ready to offer her last to the cause. "How can you subdue such a nation as this?" Asked the old Bishop-General, Leonidas Polk, on a similar occasion. That 'the good will prosper' comports with a just world. But the world is not just, and Bishop Polk is expounding upon what is righteous in a better world than this one.

It is scarcely necessary to add that, although the romance is entirely imaginary, the author has naturally drawn upon his experiences and observations during the war, both in Jackson County, Texas, and while marching with his regiment, the Second Texas Infantry, C.S.A., in Tennessee and Mississippi.

Major Thos. Preston,
late of the Second Infantry Regiment,
CONFEDERATE STATES ARMY,
Texas Volunteers, War for Southern Independence.

or The Maid of Saragoza

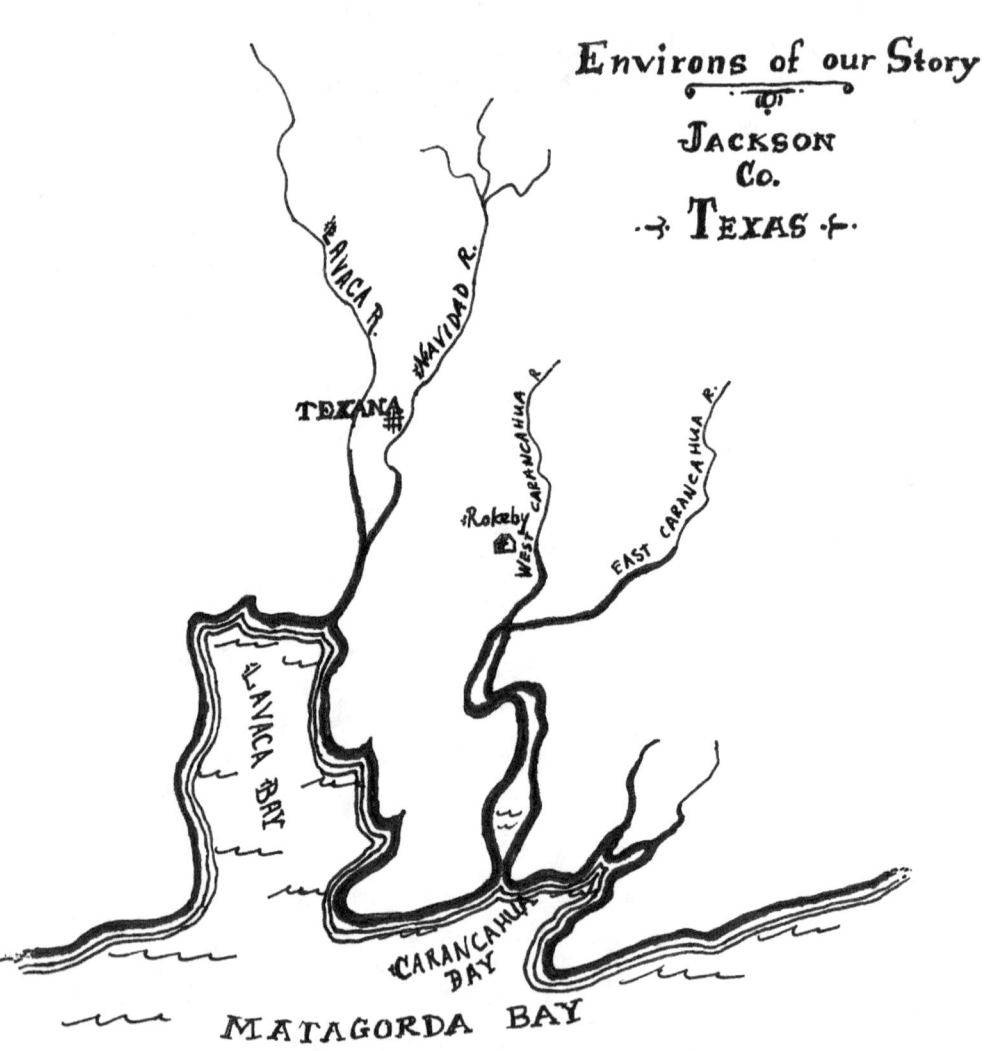

Chapter One

These silent wrecks, more eloquent than speech,
 Full many a tale of awful note impart:
Truths more severe than bard or sage can teach,
 This pomp of ruin presses on the heart.
Sad through the palm the evening breezes sigh:
 No sound of man the solitude pervades,
Where shattered forms of ancient monarchs lie,
 Mid grass-grown halls, and falling colonnades.
— PALMYRA (2nd Edition)

On a crisp autumn afternoon, in the year of 1859, three individuals were riding their horses together across the flat prairies of coastal Jackson County, Texas. Leading the way was a gentleman about fifty-five years of age, by vocation a sea captain, although he had now given up his sextant for an implement of husbandry, and by name known as John Billups. He was universally referred to as "Captain" John Billups out of respect for his nautical career. He wore his old sea captain's hat of black with a black bill. His face bore a salt and pepper beard, and deep furrows on his forehead and the sides of his face, resembling, to some extent, the weary, battered old hull of his former sailing vessels.

Following behind were two younger men. The older of the two was about twenty-five years old. He wore a military-type shell jacket and jeans, and a sharp black felt hat with a wide brim. He was dark complected and wore a neatly trimmed Vandyke beard and moustaches. This was Richard Austin Howard, who attended West Point some years ago but never graduated, nevertheless, had made while there many friends with some of the men who would play prominent roles in the great national drama that was about to open.

The youngest of the three riders was about nineteen years of age and wore the common coarse muslin clothing of a ranch hand, and a black felt hat with wide brim. He wore his hair in the usual long fashion of the times, and his face exhibited a recent beard and moustaches of dark black. Although trained as a brickmaker in his youth, and presently a ranch hand on the family ranch, he was more interested in acquiring knowledge, and was already stealing away every chance he could to his beloved books. A natural talent for artwork found him always carrying a sketch book and porte-crayon to capture any scene that struck his fancy.

He had a talent for portraiture and often delighted his friends by humorous caricatures. His education had been encouraged by his father, recently deceased, who as a self-made attorney certainly appreciated the value of book knowledge. Old John A. Wiseman, his father, had fitted all his sons with fine names of men he either knew or admired. The young man's name was Nathaniel Wright Wiseman, named for Nathaniel Wright, the Cincinnati poet and lawyer. He was called Wright by common parlance. The Wiseman family had moved from Cincinnati to Jackson County, Texas several years ago, after the death of the patriarch. Wright and the two brothers closest in age, Edward Livingston Wiseman (named for the statesman and drafter of the Louisiana civil code), and William Henry Harrison Wiseman (named for the father's friend who before he was elevated to the American Presidency, was Clerk of the Court of Common Pleas in Cincinnati while the father John served as a Judge of said Court), worked on their mother's ranch as stock-raisers and ranch hands.

The trio of riders approached the object of their journey, some Ruins which occupied an eminence which arose amidst the wind-swept Texas prairie.

"You will notice the gray stone walls, resembling the ruined Abbey's found in England, Wales and Scotland," said the old Sea Captain.

"The roof and windows have long since disappeared into decay. Notice, also, gentlemen, the grassy mound itself was surrounded by a four-foot wall of stone, now collapsed," said the Captain as he pointed to the rubble.

Richard Austin Howard and Wright Wiseman dismounted their horses and took in the bucolic scene. Grazing cattle lazily munched the prairie grass and seemed oblivious to the imposing structure dominating the pasture. On the horizon could be seen an impressive residence on the only other high eminence in the whole panorama that met the eye.

"Whose place is that?" asked Wright.

"That is 'Rokeby,' the plantation of my friend and comrade, Colonel Clark Owen," replied Captain Billups.

"Ah, he sold us our two hundred acres," said Wright.

"You are also acquainted with him, are you not, Howard?" asked the Captain.

"He has certainly been a friend and supporter of mine. My parents were of humble means. I should say, my adopted parents, who cared for me when fortune left me alone in the world and when but a small child. Colonel Owen helped me into West Point through his influence. He lends me the use of his ample library," answered Howard.

The three men walked into what would have been the interior of the ruined building. The floor of the ruins was covered in a carpet of green grass and vivid blue asters, one of the last wildflowers to bloom in the autumn. Tall, ivy-draped columns, broken and decayed and therefore of different heights, reached up towards the sky. The floor was dotted with giant corbels that once adorned the top of the ruin's massive pillars. Ivy had wrapped their tendrils up the sides of the walls, covering, and in some cases completely masking, the stone.

"These ruins are lovely and would be indescribably romantic at night with the moonbeams shining on the stone, and the owl hooting for its mate," said the impressionable Wright.

"The ivy and vines give the illusion of lush gardens hanging suspended in the sky. Not unlike the effect the famous hanging Gardens of Babylon had on the ancients," he added as he began to sketch the scene on his drawing tablet.

"Yes, there is something remarkably peaceful where nature has re-asserted herself with the works of man, and reached a kind of harmony with civilization," said the philosophic Howard.

"My belief," said the old Sea Captain, "is that these are not the works of any aboriginal peoples, but rather the works of some race from some distant locale, that had a knowledge of science."

Howard, who was aware that some believed that the French explorer, Robert Cavelier, Sieur de la Salle, had built these works, said: "These edifices display a certain level of skill and labor that the LaSalle party had neither the time nor the means to pursue. LaSalle's buildings were hewn from the logs of the forests and have long since rotted and decayed into nothing. Whoever built these works may never be known, but it was not LaSalle."

"Perhaps these walls were not built by LaSalle, but would you like to see the location of LaSalle's Fort St. Louis itself?" asked the Sea Captain with a glint in his eye.

Before Wright and Howard could answer, Captain Billups, who could not contain himself any longer, said: "It just so happens that I have recently purchased a tract of land called Dimmit's Point, down on the Lavaca River, here in Jackson County, that is the location of the famous Fort established by LaSalle in the late seventeenth century, the remnants of which were later found by De Leon, the Spanish explorer, in the early eighteenth century."

"I was under the impression that it had been conclusively proven that La Salle's fort had been located upon Garcitas Creek, in Victoria County," said Howard.

"And you would be wrong, sir. I have been making some antiquarian research on this site here in Jackson County, on the Lavaca, and it has yielded some discoveries that tie it to the great Frenchman LaSalle," said Captain Billups.

"Yes, I would like to see it," answered Howard.

"Then I shall arrange it," said the Captain joyously.

"But before we leave the Ruins, I must show you the most fascinating aspect of them," said Captain Billups, as he lifted an old carpet that was covering an old wooden door that, when opened, revealed a dark passageway leading to some underground location.

"Below the Ruins are a most extraordinary system of tunnels and subterranean passage-ways. The purposes or reasons for which seem to have eluded all investigations," said the Captain.

"Are they large enough for a man to walk in them?" asked Wright.

"Oh yes, a man of the usual height can walk quite comfortably without having to stoop. That is not what has discouraged persons from descending into them," said Captain Billups.

Howard and Wright stared into the black hole. Captain Billups, seeing that the young men's curiosity had been piqued, did not any longer keep them in suspense.

"There are many stories of strange and supernatural occurrences in these underground labyrinths," said the Captain.

"Well, nevertheless, I would like to explore these caverns sometime in the future," added Howard.

The three explored the rest of the Ruins above ground, the old Captain making several observations and commentary for the young men's edification. Eventually, the three mounted their horses and rode on to the magnificent plantation of Clark Owen that sat on a rather large hill in the distance.

Chapter Two

> I know a bank where the wild thyme blows,
> Where oxlips and the nodding violet grows,
> Quite over-canopied with luscious woodbine,
> With sweet musk-roses and with eglantine.
> — *A Midsummer Night's Dream*

The Rokeby plantation, on the "heights" as they were called, had been built by Colonel Clark Owen. To the east ran the West Carancahua creek, which drained into Carancahua Bay, which was a part of the larger Matagorda Bay. Colonel Owen was the owner of a vast stretch of territory in Jackson County. The County itself had its seat of government and commerce at Texana, a flourishing little village on the banks of the Navidad River, and a little way west of Rokeby and the other settlers along the West Carancahua. Colonel Owen, (who, incidentally, derived his title of "Colonel" as a result of his service as a soldier in the Texas War of Independence,) had constructed his house, and built his plantation, one of the grandest in all the South, adjacent to some older buildings that, architecturally, resembled the Ruins just described in the last chapter. In doing so, Colonel Owen had incorporated the old with the new. The new part of Rokeby had been built on the same plan as his ancestors had used in Kentucky, and before that, in Virginia. In fact, the Owens could trace their lineage all the way back to England, when the Owen forebears had been given, for their service to the Crown, land grants in the old Virginia colony. Each generation had furnished soldiers for America, from the American Revolutionary war down to the War for Texas Independence. Each Owen home, whether in England, Virginia, Kentucky or Texas, had been built on some high point of land that commanded the countryside around it, and most people referred to the houses as "Rokeby Heights." Having an interest in the history of the area, Owen was loath to tear down the ruinous stone structure occupying the site, and therefore, built his new edifice beside the ancient one, with a door separating the new from the old part.

Colonel Owen was, in addition to being a large farmer and stock raiser, the proprietor of a lumber and dry goods establishment which provided the Carancahua community with all necessary building materials.

In fashioning his new manor house, Owen had adopted, as has been said, the colonial style in its outlines, suggesting to the mind those happy reminiscences of elegant balls with crinoline-clad belles and handsome beaus. The magnificent Live Oaks, that measure birthdays in centuries, and which flourished on all four sides of the house, furnished a dense, shady grove to shield the inhabitants from the summer sun. The manor house's architectural beauty lay in the simplicity of construction. It was a brick structure of straight lines and plain proportions, with colonial windows and porches, and a gravel walk from the front gate to the porch. Handsome boxwood borders ran down the length of the walk. Inside the colonial appearance was carried out in the high wainscotings, heavy doors, wide halls, winding stairways and spacious rooms. Oil paintings, with portraits of Owen ancestors, hung on the walls. From the canvas looked down beautiful dames with great piles of curls and gentlemen with blue coats, brass buttons, and powdered wigs. The portrait of the little Owen child with her pet dog, could look at her father, mother, grandmother, grandfather and great-grandmother almost without turning her head.

The old-time flower garden was one of the chief ornaments of Rokeby. The winding walks, with their neatly trimmed boxwood borders, were a striking feature. The Colonel was a great lover of flowers, as had been his mother. A large, round bed marked the center of the garden and roses bloomed all through it---the moss and cluster, Giant of Battles, Shamrock, microphylla, the Harrison, and the Blush, all were cultivated as they had been on prior Owen flower gardens by prior generations extending back into Kentucky, Virginia and England.

One avenue of the graveled walks was lined with Ailanthus, or Tree of Heaven, trees. These imported Ailanthus trees were considered very rare and exotic at the time they had been planted at Rokeby. The garden contained crepe myrtle and other interesting flowering trees and shrubs. Among the species were peonies, snowballs, smoke trees, magnolia, Japan apples, crab apples, jasmines, honeysuckles, dogwoods, Rose of Sharon and Red Buds. Every tree had something planted beneath it to come up in the Spring, such as jonquils, hyacinths, snowdrops, peonies, or narcissi. The garden of ten acres required a trained gardener on hand and sometimes forty hands were brought in from the fields just to keep it in order.

Magnolia trees, with their aromatic and lovely white flowers in May and June, and Live Oaks, furnished shaded retreats. A grove of olive trees, brought from the Levant, was another novel feature of the garden at Rokeby.

Rokeby was also well known as a stock farm for beef cattle and thoroughbred horses. Just prior to the war, the plains in southern coastal Texas were literally black with cattle, and the ranches and plantations of Jackson County had reached a state of unparalleled prosperity.

As the riders dismounted and tied their horses to a hitching post, Howard said: "Let me show you gentlemen the little building that Colonel Owen is so kind to let me use."

The others dismounted and walked up to an elegant small brick building with high colonial windows and two fireplaces at either end of the building. Inside there were two rooms, one an office with a writing table, the other larger room had bookshelves built into the walls. The books sitting on the writing desk appeared to be the ones currently being read by Howard. His interests appeared to encompass a fair amount of history (both ancient and modern) combined with belles-lettres. Many of the books were adorned with bookplates, with the words "Ex Libris-Clark L. Owen" in fine old English script.

"Colonel Owen was kind enough to allow me to use the books from his library in this little building" said Howard, with a smile, as he lit with a match his Meerschaum pipe, filled with fine Turkish tobacco.

The little brick library and office stood at the base of the hill upon which Rokeby had been situated and was between the main manor house and the West Carancahua creek. A grove of trees stood on a brow of gentle declivity, that fell towards the creek. Several of the trees were ancient cedar trees, and many were tall Sycamores. Colonel Owen had even planted a little grove of orange and lemon trees, whose fruit, in the coolness of a summer evening, breathed delicious fragrance into the air.

"I am quite fond of taking one of the books and stretching out on the good grass beneath one of these Plane-trees (for so he called the Sycamores) and read. The wildlife that frequents the creek bank entertain me in their gambols. Later, after sunset, I am sometimes irresistibly drawn towards the Ruins, as I hear the wild maniacal cries of what I believe to be the Wild Man." **Note A. Wild Man of the Navidad.**

"Surely you don't believe in that old story," said Wright.

"Well, there are certainly enough of those old tales of witches and sorcery around here to keep a romance writer busy," replied Howard.

"Let me show you gentlemen the library in the main house, and offer you some refreshment," said Howard as he led the party to the manor house at Rokeby.

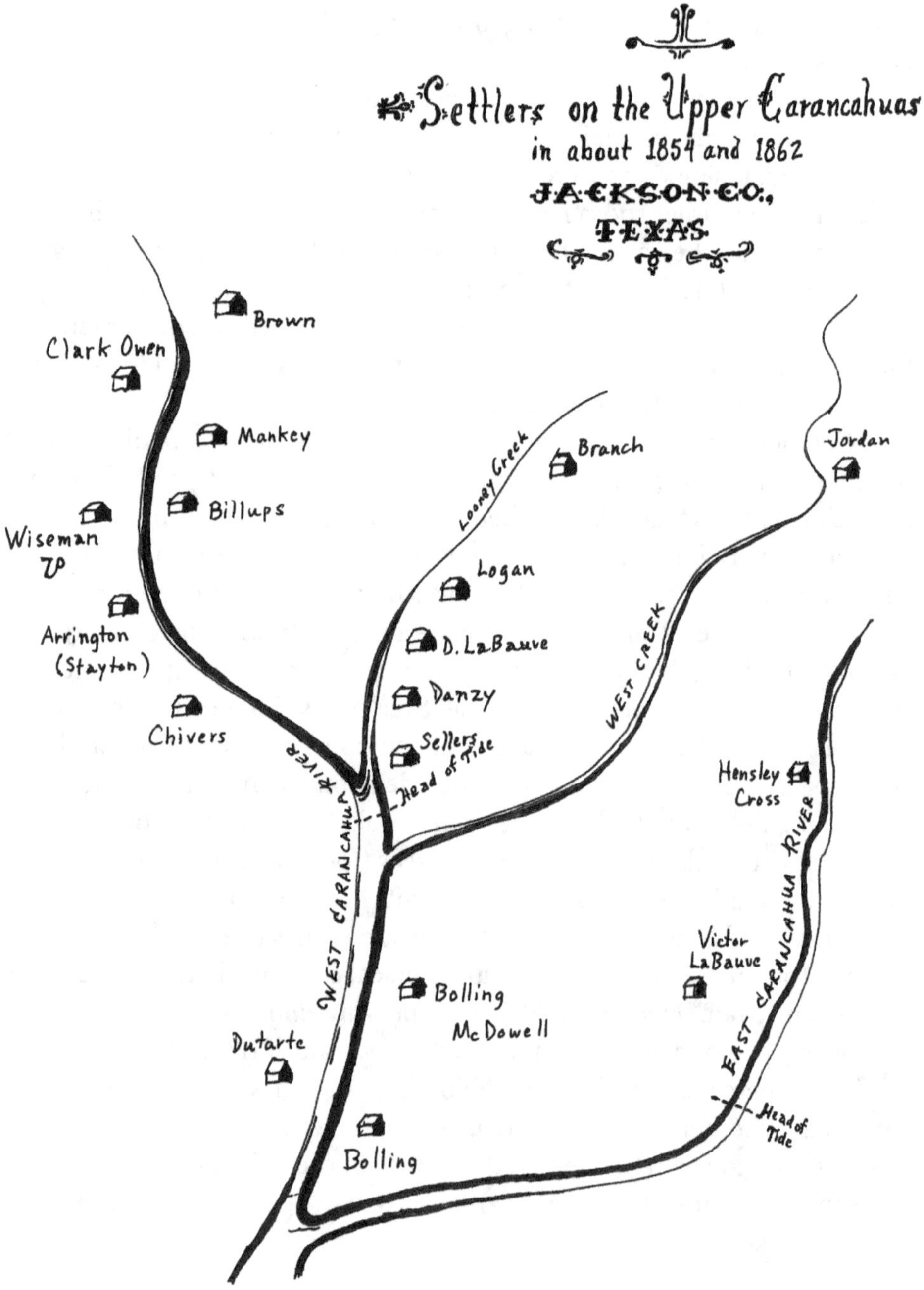

Settlers on the Upper Carancahuas
in about 1854 and 1862
JACKSON CO.,
TEXAS
Brown
Clark Owen
Mankey
Billups
Wiseman
Arrington
(Stayton)
Chivers
Looney Creek
Branch
Jordan
Logan
D. LaBauve
Danzy
Sellers
Head of Tide
WEST CREEK
Hensley
Cross
WEST CARANCAHUA RIVER
EAST CARANCAHUA RIVER
Victor
LaBauve
Bolling
McDowell
Dutarte
Bolling
Head of Tide

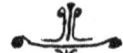

Chapter Three

'Tis said that words and signs have power,
O'er sprites in planetary hour,
But scarce I praise their venturous part,
Who tampers with such dangerous art.

— *Lay Of The Last Minstrel*

The three men walked up the hill to the grand manor house at Rokeby, where they were greeted by the Colonel himself. Colonel Clark Owen was standing under a stone archway featuring carved decorations imitating vines and leaves, and the Owen family motto: Our Right Makes Our Might. Colonel Owen pointed out the carved arch with pride, saying that the motto had been carved in all the Owen residences going back to the first one in England.

"Why Wright and Captain Billups, I believe this is your first visit to Rokeby? Come this way, let me show you my humble home! How are you enjoying this fine Autumn weather?" Colonel Owen said with a smile.

"Fair sailing weather it 'tis," replied the Sea Captain.

"Richard, I am going into Texana, if you need anything?" asked Colonel Owen.

Howard replied in the negative.

"Wright how are you and your brothers coming along with that house?" asked Colonel Owen.

"We are putting the finishing touches on it," answered Wright.

Owen had sold the widow Sarah Wiseman two hundred acres of land off the south end of his property, along the West Carancahua, and now she and her five sons and one daughter had constructed and were living in the new house.

"And a fine-looking house it is," Colonel Owen said of the Wiseman house that had been built in a grove of Live Oaks. The lumber and materials for which had come from Owen's store. The house stood a little west of the West Carancahua creek.

The design for the Wiseman home was different from the other residences in the area and reflected the tastes and influence of their former experience in the construction business in Cincinnati. The home had four sixteen by sixteen-foot square rooms, with a central hallway. There was a fireplace in each room even though the moderate Texas weather meant that only during severe cold snaps (called by the Texans a 'north-er') would the fireplaces be used. The house had a door at either end of the hallway, with a transom of three glass panes over both doors. A staircase in the center hallway led up to a half second story. On the front of the door facing north was a large brass doorknocker emblazoned with the name Wiseman on it.

"Have you decided what name you are going to call it?" asked Colonel Owen, (for no self-respecting Southerner would miss an opportunity to christen his ranch or plantation with a name of its own.)

"Yes, we are going to call it the 'Seven Up,' as our cattle brand is the 7UP brand."

"Very sensible," said Colonel Owen.

"You boys remind me," he added, with a reflective tone of voice, "that my son would be about your age now."

Colonel Owen needed not to elaborate further, for everyone in the Carancahua community knew well the sad story about Colonel Clark Owen's only son. Colonel Owen and his wife had suffered the tragic experience of having an unknown person kidnap their only son, about twenty years prior to the time of our tale.

There was no ransom demand, nor was there any trace of the little boy. Some suspected that Indians, or perhaps the gypsies, had taken him for inclusion into their tribe. Others said the five- year-old had wandered into the Carancahua and been swept away to the Gulf. Colonel Owen always maintained that the boy was only missing and would someday return. The Colonel was raising two beautiful daughters, but without a male heir to assume the care and maintenance of the large plantation of Rokeby, it was likely that Rokeby would be sold at Colonel Owen's death.

Colonel Owen's kidnapped son had entered this world under auspicious circumstances. Flora, one of the trusted servants at Rokeby, was young Master Owen's nurse. "Miss Flora," as she was often called, in addition to being a faithful member of the Owen household, was a well-known "Seer" and practitioner of a benign form of African necromancy, or astrology, and she was regularly consulted by persons of both races, for information she supposedly possessed.

Flora, and others endowed with this gift, could tell a person's destiny by a reading of the celestial heavens at the time of a person's birth. In the instance of young Master Owen, she predicted that two ages would present danger to the boy: age five and age twenty-five.

It was at age five that the boy disappeared, and even though it was well known that Flora adored the child, suspicion naturally followed when the child in fact had disappeared at one of the ages predicted by

Flora as posing a danger to him. It was well remembered, however, that Flora would frequently rock with the child under the shade of the trees at Rokeby, and that she would customarily stroll the child to the location of a nearby knoll, on which stood a large old Live Oak tree, (that had been struck by a lightning bolt, and was partially riven in two,) that overlooked the Ruins. The knoll upon which the gigantic Oak stood, was not far from Rokeby, and on the seat beneath the tree, which had been erected there by Colonel Owen, Flora and the child would rock, and look down upon the Ruins, and out over the scenic panorama in the distance. An English Ivy vine which had been planted at the base of the tree, wrapped its graceful tendrils around the Oak's sturdy yet damaged knotted trunk.

Those who argued Flora's innocence reminded Colonel Owen of the stories Flora would tell her young charge: "This tree, young Master Owen, has magical powers, as sure as your two-foot high, little one, and the Injuns that used to sit beneath it, jes like we're a doin', used its leaves and bark to heal their wounds and make medicine. Do you even know what I mean, by 'magic'? A wise old Owl told me about those Injuns using this here tree. Yessir, they used to dance their wild dances, in their eagle feathers and animal skins, with all their skin painted. Do you believe that little Master?" and she would smile as she let the little boy down to play on the ground.

Flora loved to sing her songs and rhymes to young Master Owen, and one of these stories she delighted to tell the boy, that everybody remembered, was the story of what she called 'The Riven Oak and the Ivy.' The story went thusly:

In the Wilderness, long before the first settlers placed their first dusty footprints on this prairie, stood a mighty Oak. So majestic was he that all who came that way paused to admire his strength and beauty, and all the other trees of the wilderness acknowledged him to be their Monarch. Now the Ivy loved the Oak tree and wrapped her graceful tendrils around his sturdy and knotted trunk. The Oak tree told the Ivy the pretty stories about the clouds, the birds, and the stars. These were stories the Oak tree heard from the wind that loitered about his lofty head.

Whenever the storms came, the Oak would say to the Ivy: 'Cling close to me, little vine, and no harm would befall you! See how strong I am.'

The years went by, Spring, Summer, Autumn, Winter and over again, and decades passed, and the Ivy was no longer a weak little vine. The Ivy stretched far up among the Oak tree's lower branches. And the Oak tree loved the Ivy.

Then one day, the Oak whispered to the Ivy: 'There is a terrible storm coming over the hills and plains, the East wind told me so, and the birds fly low, and the sky is dark!'

And the Storm King hurled his mighty thunderbolts at the Oak tree, and the brave monarch of the forest was split practically in two.

And the Ivy said to the Oak: 'You are riven!' 'Aye,' said the Oak, 'My end has come, I am shattered and useless!'

'I will bind up your wounds and nurse you back to health and vigor,' said the Ivy.

And then the Ivy would tell the Oak all the stories she had learned from the crickets, the bees, the butterflies, and the mice, while she was a humble little vine and played at the foot of the majestic Oak. They were not as heroic as the tales of the winds and the clouds and the stars, but they were far sweeter, for they were tales of contentment and humility and love.

And the Oak lived on — and not one person saw the havoc of the years or the ruin of the tempest, but only the glory of the Oak tree's age.

Despite that Flora loved the little Owen boy almost as if he had been her own kith and kin, as was previously alluded to, natural suspicion fell upon her after her augury was recalled. After a thorough investigation, Flora was cleared of any responsibility in the boy's disappearance. Nevertheless, Colonel Owen dismissed Flora from Rokeby, earning a scathing curse from the old woman, (although she made it clear that she loved, and would always love, the little Owen heir), specifically, she predicted that bad tidings would befall the House of Owen. Flora was sold to the neighboring plantation of Victor LaBauve, and never again did Flora set foot upon Rokeby Heights.

Chapter Four

You must of necessity believe that there are women
Of supernatural science, framers of nocturnal
Incantations, who can turn the world upside down.
— PETRONIUS

The locality of the Navidad and Lavaca rivers, which converged a little below where the county seat of Texana was located, and including the Carancahua creeks to the east, had long been a region celebrated for wonderful instances of magic and unexplained events. So much so, that it might be considered the Thessaly of America.

As such, when Captain John Billups left the seafaring life and became a resident of the area several years prior to the time of our tale, he examined all things with intense curiosity.

The belief in the supernatural powers of certain women on the plantations was very prevalent. It was a common article of faith among the Negroes that these enchantresses could, by nocturnal incantations and magic ceremonies, "draw down the moon." Their powers were consulted in such matters of the healing of diseases, the improvement of crops, and a host of other problems that confronted these hardy Texans.

Captain Billups had promised to show young Howard and Wright Wiseman the land he had recently purchased on the Lavaca River, known as Dimmit's Point, and which, (according to the Captain), contained the site of the Sieur de LaSalle's Fort St. Louis.

Consequently, Captain Billups, Richard Howard, and Wright Wiseman resolved on the next day to ride over to the supposed location of the remnants of LaSalle's settlement.

While on the way, Wright inquired concerning the topic of the supernatural incidents, such as the Wild Man of the Navidad, discussed the day before. Howard, who in addition to his wild, headstrong nature, had another, more quiet side to him. He would shut himself away from the busy world and read through the well-stocked library of classical literature at Rokeby. It was then the student of the classics that observed: "Pliny, the Roman, considered the belief in magic as the combined effect of the operation of three powerful causes: medicine, superstition, and the mathematical arts. One might add music, to which the ancients ascribed the most miraculous powers. The belief in the supernatural powers of music and pharmacy ascends to the earliest ages of poetry and appear to have been a favorite topic for the ancients' social hours."

"The Negroes on the plantations in the vicinity of the Ruins imagine that every object around them has been changed by incantation from its natural shape, that the trees in the country and the birds singing in their boughs, are human beings, in the disguise of leaves and feathers. They expect statues and images to walk, the walls to speak, cattle to utter prophetic voices, and oracles from the morning sky," he added.

Wright asked: "But what about the strange cries and sounds that emanate from the Ruins, are these attributable to the Wild Man? Who or what is the Wild Man?"

"No one knows exactly what he is, son," said Captain Billups. "He lives in the heavily wooded thickets along the Navidad and Lavaca rivers, and probably, to a lesser degree, along the two Carancahuas. He frequents sweet potato patches and corn fields, to take a few potatoes and ears," he added.

"On certain nights, when the moon is in a particular phase, he will come out," said the Captain, "Occasionally, he will actually enter a house (for windows were often opened at night in the summertime) and will take a loaf of bread from the pantry. Oftentimes, valuables will be visible by the moonlight, but never taken. Guard dogs seem mysteriously uninterested in the stranger."

"And what do the Negroes think about him?" asked Wright.

"Oh, they want nothing to do with him. You cannot get one of them to accompany you to the Ruins, a favorite spot for the Wild Man, except for that eccentric witch of a woman that used to sit out under that old riven Oak tree on the ground overlooking the Ruins," remarked Captain Billups.

"You are speaking of this Flora, the former domestic of Colonel Owen's?" asked Howard.

"Yes, that hag, and her crazy incantations," laughed the Captain, "apart from her, you cannot get one of the darkies to accompany you to the Ruins, said to be a favorite spot of the Wild Man. Although, I have never seen him there in any of my antiquarian research. The Negroes generally refer to him as THAT THING THAT COMES, as if to name him would conjure him up."

As the three men rode further towards Captain Billups's recent acquisition, they saw an older Negro out in a field trying to lasso a roan horse that was splashed with mud and had curious tangles of briers in its mane. To the three riders, it appeared the horse had been running in pastures, partly marshy and containing brier patches.

Captain Billups recognized the man attempting to catch the horse as one of the Owen servants, named Joe. He watched the man eventually gain control of the horse and get a bridle on him.

"Come on, you, I'se got you now!" shouted the pursuer triumphantly.

"Joe, what are you up to?" called out the Captain.

"Good morn Cap'n. Dis hoss done been witch ridden all night," said Joe.

"What the devil are you talking about?" asked the Captain with a wry smile.

"Oh, dis here hoss has been tak'n by a witch an ridden all night. See dees knots an tangles?" said Joe with complete sincerity, as he pointed to the curious tangles in the horse's mane, "dis here is witches' stirrups."

"Joe you black rascal, I reckon the horse probably ran off when you were supposed to be watching and wandered among the wet ground and briers," scolded the Captain.

Billups turned to Wright and Howard, smiled, and said: "the Negroes are extremely superstitious. Witches and ghosts — 'sperits' in Negro parlance — are the chief subjects of their superstitious faith and awe."

"Do they find witches amongst their womenfolk?" asked Howard.

"No, not really, their witches are a sort of wood-sprite, who like to perform strange and mischievous pranks, like riding horses all night!" said the Captain as he looked back at old Joe.

Joe, taking the Captain's words to indicate a complete vindication of his explanation, went on to say: "Cap'n Billups, doan go near de Ruins at night, des sperits there sho enuf," with a serious look of concern on his face.

Captain Billups turned to two younger men and continued with his lecture: "Every deserted house, almost every secluded and weird-looking corner of the forest or field, was supposed to be haunted by some spirit which jealously guarded its peculiar premises," said the Captain.

"I must admit," said Howard, "when I was a boy, this feature of the Negro superstition, made me, when listening to their stories, feel very uncomfortable," said Howard.

"Doan you nuvver let a sperit see you. Ef he once sees you, he gwine to allus ha'nt you," chimed in Joe.

The riders came to a location where a well-remembered duel was fought years ago, and one of the combatants was killed. Captain Billups used this occasion to make an observation: "There appears to be a difference of opinion among the Negroes as to whether these spots were haunted. One side holds to the opinion that every locality where a violent death

or The Maid of Saragoza

has occurred is always and necessarily haunted by the spirit of the person who had so suffered."

"Ah reckon only when a wicked murder ha' been done, will you find a sperit. No white gen'elman what was killed in a fair fight would 'sturb niggers what hadn't done him no harm," opined Joe.

As the three riders rode on, Joe joined them on their journey. At length they arrived at the object of their quest.

Chapter Five

An antiquary went to pry.
    For burrows, mounds, and tumuli
And by a dike erect alone
    To his delight he found a stone
With characters most rude inscribed
    Yet legible
        KEE
            PONT
                HISS
                    IDE

The Antiquary: An Old story in a New Shape

The three riders and Joe trailing somewhat behind, rode toward the Lavaca river, passing cactus and grazing cattle and little groves of Live Oak trees, called Mottes, until they had reached Captain Billups's newly acquired land.

"I have found many hewn stones and curious objects while trenching the ground, several of which I have sent as specimens to my learned friends, and to various antiquarian societies of which I am a member. Here, we have reached a truly remarkable spot. I am surprised I was able to convince Colonel Owen to let go of this tract, although he drove a hard bargain, I knew that Dimmit's Point was an important piece of ground."

"Truly it commands a fine view," said Howard, as he gazed on the gentle declivity that led down to the waters of the Lavaca river, with the ancient oaks along the bank draped in Spanish moss.

"True but it is not for the prospect that I brought you hither, do you see nothing else remarkable? Nothing on the surface of the ground?" said Captain Billups.

"Why yes, I do see something like a ditch, indistinctly marked …" replied Howard.

"Indistinctly! — pardon me but the indistinctness must be in your powers of vision — nothing can be more plainly traced. An arroyo, or dry ditch, leading from the high ground down to the banks of the Lavaca, just as it is described by the historian of LaSalle's expedition, Joutel. Fools and idiots have ploughed up the land, and, like beasts and ignorant savages, have thereby obliterated two sides of the square, and greatly injured the third, but you see the fourth side is quite entire," said Captain Billups.

The Sea Captain proceeded to explain about the Redoubt that was, at least to him, very distinct: "You must know," he said, "our Texas antiquaries have been greatly divided about the local situation of the Fort which LaSalle established when he came to Texas in search of the mouth of the Mississippi."

"Why did LaSalle deem the mouth of the Mississippi to be important?" asked Wright.

"LaSalle was convinced that whoever controlled the mouth of the Mississippi, would control the destiny of the country. He was bound and determined to wrest it away from Spain, and give it to his native France," said Captain Billups.

"Any individual that reads Joutel's account of this settlement and visits Dimmit's Point will be thoroughly convinced that it is the site of Old Fort St. Louis. Why, the fact that Fort St. Louis was built on the Lavaca river has been undisputed for over fifty years. Such eminent historians as Parkman, Bancroft, G.P. Garrison, H.S. Thrall and numerous other historians all place Fort St. Louis on the Lavaca river. Many specifically name the fort site as Dimmit's Point," lectured the Captain.

He continued: "When LaSalle explored the rivers and bays of Texas, he made several interior trips, all in vain trying to find the Mississippi River. LaSalle established Fort St. Louis on the Lavaca River in 1685. He and his men made the most of the situation. The little French colony at Fort St. Louis dwindled down to a mere handful. Finally, in 1689, four years after the colony had made their settlement on the Lavaca, most of the survivors were slain by the Karankawa Indians." **Note B. Karankawa Indians.**

"But Professor Bolton has advanced a theory that LaSalle built Fort St. Louis on Garcitas Creek in Victoria County," said Howard.

"Hold on now sir, trim your sails, I've not done yet. He bases his theory on an old map by Cardenas which is not authoritative. Cardenas missed the names of almost every river he visited along the Texas coast. He mistook the Navidad for the San Marcos, the Colorado for the Trinidad, why if an explorer made as many mistakes as Cardenas did, he should not be considered an authority. If he made these mistakes, it is reasonable to conclude he was mistaken on the location of Fort St. Louis at Garcitas Creek. Professor Bolton bases most of his claims on the diary of and map of Cardenas. He admits that Cardenas missed naming all the rivers, yet he wishes to use him to prove that a tradition and historic fact for hundreds of years is not true," said the Sea Captain.

"Undoubtedly so," was all that Howard could say.

"DeLeon, that great Spanish explorer, who came along later in the next century, described seeing the location where the French had built their settlement. There was an arroyo, that is, a dry ditch, that flowed into a bay. The water was salty, and it had tides. The fort was a Redoubt, and there were six houses solidly built of ship's timber surrounding it. Look before you, you see the fabled wall of that redoubt," said the Captain as he proudly pointed to the supposed earthworks.

"What would you say, Howard, if the memorable scene where the noble Robert Cavalier, Sieur de LaSalle, built his fort and unfurled the French flag with its Fleur de Lis, and treated with the heathen savage Karankawa, should happen to be the very spot called Dimmit's Point, the property of the obscure and humble individual who now speaks to you?"

Then, having paused a little, to suffer his guests to digest a communication so important, he resumed his disquisition in a higher tone: "Yes, my good friends, I am greatly deceived if this place does not correspond with all the marks of that celebrated place of action. It was near a body of water into which an arroyo drained, which was a body of salt water, which had tides, there was a Redoubt, with six low mounds on which sat the six log houses---lo! Yonder they are. It is astonishing how blind we professed antiquaries sometimes are. I was afraid to say a word about it until I had secured the ground, Colonel Owen was a hard bargainer. At length, I am almost ashamed to say it—I even traded my good corn-land as part of the deal, for this barren spot. But then it is a matter of importance to Texas, and when the scene of so celebrated an event became my own, I was overpaid. I began to trench the ground, to see what might be discovered, and the third day, sir, we found a stone, carved to be a sacrificing spoon, used no doubt by the Sulpician priests, and bearing the letters A-J-L-L which may stand, without much violence, for 'Abbe Jean Loc Leman.'"

"Certainly, you are aware, sir, that the Sieur de LaSalle's brother Jean was a Priest of the Sulpician Order, and accompanied his brother to America. Now this redoubt. ..."

A voice from behind interrupted his description, and it was old Joe, who had finally caught up with the other riders, on his jaded, witch-ridden mount.

"Doubt here, Doubt dere ... Doubt Doubt ebry whar ... I know bout dis, dis wha d'you call, 'Doubt'? Dis here Doubt was built by me, Sneaky Pete, Amos Jordan and some of de mason boys, you know, de ones dat built de dike. Marse Owen had us out here ... nigh ten years ago, an we

or The Maid of Saragoza

made dis here ... Doubt," said Joe.

"Redoubt, you old fool. It was here before you were born, and will be here after you are hanged, man!" said the Captain, whose face was one of mild aggravation, as he added: "What the devil do you know about this?"

"Jes dat me and some of de boys, jes to have a laff at Amos Jordan, who loved to hunt squirrels, an afta dat fix a big pot o' squirrel stew, and afta we wuz quate drunk, we'd sit around the pot wit de others, an take turns dippin' outta de pot, de pieces o' de cooked squirrel, and de 'winner' wuz de nigger who ladled out the head, fo he got de honna of cracking de head open an' suckin' out de brains. (Well, you know de brains is de most tasty pat). An jes for a laff de mason boys carved out a dippin spoon with de letters A-J-L-L — that's Amos Jordan's Long Ladle. An if ye dig up dis here ... Doubt, which looks like you've already started, you'll find it buried thar," said Joe.

The Captain's face resembled that of a young child whose carefully constructed house of cards has just been blown down by a malicious companion.

"There is some mistake about this," said the Captain.

"Naw ah don't hev nuttin to do wit mistakes, dey bring mischances. Lawd bless y' honna, nobody'll know a word about it from me, more'n if de little mound had been der since Noah's flood. But Lawd, dey tell me y'honna has given Cunnel Owen acre fo acre of good corn land fo dis barren knoll."

The Sea Captain muttered some indignant words of which only the word "scoundrel" could be distinctly understood, then in a louder tone said: "Never mind, Joe — it is all a mistake."

"Lawd, dats what ah tol' em, dat Cap'n Billups wud nevah done sich a foolish thing as to give good ground fo a patch o' ground dats likely to be under water fo de betta part of. ..."

"Away with you, Joe! And take your witch-ridden nag ... and ride back to Rokeby. And I will thank you not to be spreading your d____d nonsensical story over half the country," interrupted the Captain.

With that, Joe departed, and the three riders rode to their respective homes.

Chapter Six

> But sweeter still than this, than these, than all,
> Is first and passionate love — it stands alone,
> Like Adam's recollection of his fall,
> The tree of knowledge has been plucked — all's Known —
> And life yields nothing further to recall.
>
> *Don Juan, Canto CXXVII*

The forest trees along the Carancahuas are in Autumn unmatched in the splendor of their foliage and are as splendid as the forests of any other portion of the continent. The days spent in the woods under the reign of Indian Summer, is indeed a luxury. From morning until night, the sun shines and meets no interrupting cloud. The bluish-gray haze of the atmosphere hangs over hill and plain and river, making the distant dreamy, and what is near very beautiful. The warm beams give new life to the body, while the glories of the landscape awaken in the mind all its reminiscences of youth and evoke all its poetic association.

The Carancahuas, sometimes referred to as rivers, are really bayous, being bodies of salt water, except during the rainy season when they really become rivers, draining thousands of acres of the South Texas plains country. The trees that border the streams are draped with the lovely gray moss. The moss is a lichen growing on the barks of the trees in long, flowing bunches, with little gray leaves growing in clusters. The West and East Cararcahuas come together in a bend, forming the Carancahua Bay, which is an inlet of Matagorda Bay.

On an Autumn afternoon, there is just enough breeze to lift the curl on the brow of the beautiful being who sits beside you, and to rustle the crisp leaves on the branches above your head. Ever and anon the leaves come whirling down to unite with the leafy mantle that is spread over the ground. The dropping of the nuts on the dry leaves, or the rapid passage of the squirrel, anxious to leave you to the enjoyment of your emotions, or even the cawing of the crow, as he sits on the topmost limb of a tall poplar, are sounds that the heart does not willingly or soon forget. Occasionally a whirl in the breeze sets the leaves in motion, and, as the tiny whirl goes by you, you are forced to think of those coming gales, of which it is the herald, that will, ere long, roar like an ocean, and strip all the foliage off, and leave the limbs of the trees bare and bleak, until Spring, with her sweet, warm lips, shall kiss them into fresh life and beauty.

It was on just such an Autumn day that young Wright Wiseman and Kate Dandridge happened to meet each other for the first time. They were nearly the same age, about eighteen years, when they were both attending a Tournament, one of the most picturesque events that were popular in those days.

It was still a tradition, in parts of the South, to stage these pageants, which were really the last vestiges of the chivalric tradition. Harking back to Roman times, and even Trojan times, these exercises were of a martial nature. They were quite common during the feudal ages and served a two-fold purpose. They were used to train the young men in the skills necessary in battle, and they also inculcated respect, reverence and love towards the fair sex. While it armed its knights and squires in iron, it mantled the female sex in the strong panoply of virtue. It taught the youth of both sexes to set marriage before them as an honorable estate, to be entered upon after a series of trials had proved the young paladin was worthy of the object of his choice, and his fair one faithful. As the poet writes:

> Then was Love no idle dream,
> Lightly come and lightly past,
> But a pure and holy beam
> Burning brightly to the last.
> Leading on the young and brave
> To the charge of steel-clad men,
> To the peril of the wave,
> To the dragon in his den.

At this Tournament, the "knights" did not wear the iron suits and chainmail that harkened back to medieval times, but the attire was, nevertheless, of great importance. The rider, dressed in white britches and shirt, would offer a badge of the colors of his bright sash to a flattered female who, if her knight were successful, would be crowned the Queen of Love and Beauty. Some riders wore a plumed hat and matching colored sash. Some wore a green tunic.

The location was a meadow of good flat green grass, large enough for the riders to gallop eighty yards. The lance, made from a barrel of a shotgun, was about seven feet tall. The object was to spear certain rings, which were suspended from two posts. The rings were placed at equidistant intervals along the course, and the rider galloped about twenty-seven yards, before he made each try. The Texans referred to the revival of the Medieval Tournament as "ridin' and ringin'" or "threading the needle on horseback."

It may be fashionable for the modern age to sneer at these imitations of feudal times, but it must be remembered that it was altogether a wholesome pastime and brought together from distant places the young and the old of both sexes and served to perfect the elegant accomplishments of horsemanship. And horsemanship was, to a Texan, very important. The Texans, whose creed was to never walk anywhere when they could ride, had difficulty in fielding infantry regiments, when the war finally did break out in 1861, so much greater was the Texans' preference to be a horse soldier in the cavalry arm of the service.

Young Wright Wiseman was participating as one of the "Knights" and Kate Dandridge was one of the unmarried young ladies who were candidates for "Maids of Honour," and who would be selected by the Queen, (to be crowned by the champion of the ring competition).

The Knights, comprised of the young men of the surrounding area, were to prove their ability to bear the sword and the lance, in the young ladies' behalf, if such necessity should arise.

The course, alluded to previously, featured three rings that began with a diameter of an inch-and-a-quarter and descended in size to about an inch. It was a true feat of horsemanship to ride at full speed passing between the posts and bearing off the ring upon the point of a lance.

The Knights were nobly mounted, and dressed as previously described, and assumed names which were called off by the Herald: "The Knight of Lochinvar," or "of the Templar," "The Black Knight," "The Knight of Templestowe," "Roderick Dhu," and so on, to the end of the list. A short recitation of the rules of the Tournament were then read by the Herald. Music sounded and the Knights turned and passed out of sight of the ladies, concealed by trees. The Herald gave a signal, and the Knights came one after the other, on their coursers, some bearing away the ring, to the delight and applause of the spectators, and some having varying degrees of success.

The next competition concerned an exhibition of the use of the lasso, or lariat. This talent came practically natural to the young men of Texas. The Knight would again ride at full speed, and attempt to throw the lasso over a wild horse or calf, released on signal by the assistants of the Herald.

At length, the Black Knight, (who was known to all as William Stayton, whose family's ranch was just to the south of the Seven Up Ranch,)

or The Maid of Saragoza

having taken the ring five times and having lassoed the calf three times, was crowned the champion, and was entitled to select the Queen of Love and Beauty. The Queen of Love and Beauty in turn selected from the unmarried young ladies three Maids of Honour who made professions of devotion to the three Knights deemed to be next in skill to the Black Knight. These Knights then professed their willingness to conquer the invaders of their country in defense of the women.

That evening a Grand Ball was given for the people attending the Tournament. Flattering speeches were made, and toasts given "to the women of Texas---the safeguards of our honor and our liberty." It was at this Grand Ball that young Wright Wiseman and Kate Dandridge realized they were falling in love.

Miss Kate Dandridge was the petite, intelligent young daughter of old Hastings Dandridge, a veteran of the War for Texas Independence. Kate had been blessed with a superior intellect and a sharp wit. She had long, flowing black hair, "black as the raven's wing," and a face, if not classically beautiful, certainly was considered pleasant, with ivory skin, and attractive hazel eyes. To Wright, who had been struck by Cupid's arrow for the first time, Kate was the most beautiful creature that the sun ever shone on. Her winsome personality charmed her contemporaries, who commented on her intelligence and humor and noted her slender, diminutive girlish stature. The eighteen-year-old had cast a spell on Wright, and she had been flattered by the attention he was giving to her.

In the days and weeks following the Tournament, Kate would arrange to sit beside Wright to study her school lessons. Wright would arrange to walk by Kate's house while she sat on the front porch. The barn dances given, as the days shortened and the nights became cooler, found them arriving with friends from childhood, but as the evening wore on, eventually spending time talking and dancing with each other. Soon those childhood friends they had arrived with, were left to their own devices. Indeed, the two were passing into that next stage in the pageant that is life. Christmas time found them together by the fireside, exchanging gifts.

Wright was constantly amazed by Kate's inexhaustible fund of optimism.

"Why are you always so happy?" asked Wright.

"Because of what I do on Sunday," was her reply.

This puzzled Wright, at first, but then he recalled her deep and abiding faith as a witness for Christ. Indeed, several years before meeting Wright, Kate had undergone a conversion experience. Far more than just an unfailing optimism, her faith pervaded every facet of her life. She told

Wright how her old self was gone, and Christ had given her a new life.

Wright had not known her before her conversion, but he certainly had no reason to doubt her statements: it was evident in everything she did or said whether great or small. She would chide Wright sometimes, for instance when he would say he "hated" someone or something.

"But are there not some instances where it is appropriate to hate?"

"No, never," was the earnest reply.

Wright asked the old familiar questions that mankind has asked for untold generations: "How does one know he is saved?" To this question Kate patiently explained that there was no flash of inspiration or other-worldly manifestation. It was just a feeling of calmness and certainty, and a notion that sin and temptation was gradually disappearing from one's life.

Kate made it plain to Wright, as the young couple continued their courtship and made plans for future matrimonial life, that she would have only a Christian for a husband. This did not cause concern for Wright, as the young poet and ranch hand had even considered the clergy as a livelihood.

The young couple were tested when Kate went off to study at a Young Ladies' Seminary located a great distance from Jackson County, located in fact, outside the State of Texas, in one of our northern states. The modes of transportation and Kate's meager finances made visits home few and seldom. Now, it was during Kate's summer vacations that Wright and Kate cherished their time together.

Ah Summer! How this happy season of the year brought to Wright's mind, the carefree, indolent, long Summer days spent with Kate Dandridge! Early each morning, as Wright rode his horse past Kate's parent's home, heading for the fields and pastures, he would whistle a tune while passing her open window. Later, Kate would tell him how grand it was, to lay in bed with the first golden rays of the morn peeping through the windows, and hear her beloved's song, reassuring her that all was well. Then of an evening, after the chores and cares of the day were done, the couple would sit on the front porch, gazing into each other's eyes, and talk of their future lives together, for both young persons had made the commitment to spending their lives together.

Thus passed the Summer days that were firmly impressed upon Wright's memories.

or The Maid of Saragoza

The Riven Oak and the Ivy

Chapter Seven

What are these?
So wither'd and so wild in their attire,
That look not like the inhabitants o' earth,
And yet are on't?

— *Macbeth*

John Adams Brackenridge and Colonel Clark Owen had both been friends for several years prior to the summer of 1860, the time we have now arrived at in our story. They shared some common interests, and
their children were roughly the same age. The two men even jointly hired a governess from New York to teach the French language to their children.

John Adams Brackenridge was a lawyer by profession, who had come from Indiana to Texas some years ago. Brackenridge had come to Texas to speculate in real estate, which he saw as a great opportunity. The time would come, thought Brackenridge, that the real estate in Jackson County, currently a bargain, would increase many folds in value as new settlers from the East arrived.

The senior Brackenridge passed on to his two sons, Tom and George, this mania for real estate speculation. The two sons, who were in their early twenties, were temperamentally opposites, and would both take opposite sides in the war that was still a distant prospect in the summer of 1860.

Old John Adams Brackenridge, however, secretly coveted the fine plantation of his friend Clark Owen. The Elder Brackenridge had offered to buy out Owen after his son had disappeared, but Owen had declined. Colonel Owen still harbored a belief that his missing son would return and take his rightful position as master of Rokeby Heights.

On this summer day in 1860, John Adams Brackenridge and Colonel Owen were inspecting some cattle branding being performed on Owen's plantation, and the two men were riding past the Ruins, when they noticed on the rise overlooking the Ruins, an individual seated beneath the ancient Live Oak that was covered in English Ivy. When they rode on a little further, they recognized that the person was the seer, Flora, Owen's former servant.

"I thought that you had thrown her off your property, Colonel," said

Brackenridge.

Colonel Owen did not reply and had a pained expression on his face. He guided his horse on a path to take him closer to where the old harpy was seated. Up to the eminence he rode.

"Woman," cried out Owen, "what business do you have here?"

"This is the place I loved to sit and rock young Master Owen for many an hour and sing my songs and rhymes."

"Yes, yes, I know. And you have also been told to leave this property and to never return."

"Colonel, when I was banished, you remember I cursed you and the House of Owen. However, I never leveled this curse at young Master Owen, my charge, whom I loved as a son, and I will cherish the day when I once again see his face and know he has taken his rightful possession of Rokeby Heights. But as to you, a curse I put upon your life for banishing me unjustly!"

"Woman I do not fear your threats any more than I believe your lies. But if you know where my son is, how he fares, then for pity's sake, tell me?"

"I just know he will return, that he is alive, but I do not know where he is to be found. He will return to make the wrong into right."

"Begone yon hateful witch, your words make no sense. Do not antagonize me and take care not to let our paths cross again. The next time I will bring the sheriff and have you punished for disobeying my injunction."

"Once more did I crave," said the Negro seer, "to sit beneath this old Oak, and listen to the sound of the wind as it rustles through the leaves and branches, although time has taken its toll on this here tree, and it is falling apart and shields me less and less, from the summer sun. Yet the Ivy vine helps to bind up its wounds."

"Begone witch, when I ride back by here, or I will have you thrown in the county jail," replied Owen.

Colonel Owen and Brackenridge rode on to the appointed place of cattle branding.

Owen being the kindhearted, Christian Gentleman he was, had no idea that John Adams Brackenridge was a false friend, and nurtured in his heart the desire to become the master of Rokeby Heights.

Brackenridge's son Tom had formed a partnership with another merchant, James Bates, known as Brackenridge and Bates. The general merchandise firm of Brackenridge and Bates had provided the people of Jackson County with sundry articles necessary to keep their ranches and plantations operating smoothly for several years prior to 1860. By shrewd dealings and long hours of labor, the Yankee merchants were able to provide a fine livelihood for their families and were slowly beginning to be accepted into the higher social circles of society in Jackson County. However, events that were transpiring would drive a wedge between "Brackenridge and Bates", and most of their fellow citizens.

The election of Abraham Lincoln in late 1860 had been a signal to the South that the Northern states had adopted a hostile position towards the South. Even before the firing on Fort Sumter in April of '61 and Lincoln's call for troops to invade the South, Texas had voted to leave the Union and align herself with the forming Southern Confederacy.

The issues of the day were also causing internal problems between family members in Jackson County. In the Brackenridge family, brother Tom had joined with the secessionists, while brother George refused to volunteer for Confederate service. With the Brackenridge brothers, loyalty to a cause was purely a matter of business.

"Say Tommy," asked the cool calculating George, "you know there is a war coming on?"

"The war about state's rights between the North and the South?" said Tom.

" No, I mean the one about the nigger between the North and the South," said George.

"What side are you going to take, George?"

"You go join the Confederates, and I'll join the Union army," said George.

"What, brother fight brother?" said Tom.

"It is purely a matter of business," said George.

"But which side is going to win?" asked Tom.

"Who can tell what side is going to win, Tom. Nobody knows the answer to that question. If your side wins, you help me. If my side wins, I'll help you. That's business," said George.

Chapter Eight

My library was Dukedom large enough.

— *The Tempest*

The love affair between Wright Wiseman and Miss Kate Dandridge continued after Kate had resumed her course of studies in the North. The couple wrote long letters to each other, to try and assuage the anguish at being separated from one another. The letters were filled with the typical juvenile musings between young persons, with topics such as the names of future dear children, the books that were being read, the lyrics to the popular songs of that time, and pledges and promises to be "thine forever."

Miss Kate Dandridge was determined to be a teacher and was immersing herself with the great works of literature, from both modern and ancient authors.

Wright's interests had previously been limited to such mundane subjects as the building trades, raising and racing horses, hunting, and fishing. At least once a year Wright would join his brothers and some hired hands, on a cattle drive that typically took place over the "Old Trail" that led through Jackson County thence eastward towards New Orleans. The cattle drivers had to swim, ford, or ferry their beeves across many rivers and bayous. Proceeding eastward from Jackson County, these cattle-drivers had to cross the Colorado, Brazos, Buffalo Bayou, Trinity, San Jacinto, Neches, and Big Bayou rivers, then finally cross the Sabine, into Louisiana. Once in Louisiana, the Calcasieu and the Mississippi had to be overcome to reach the stockyards of New Orleans.

Thus, Wright and his fellow cowhands learned how to live and work out in the wild, knowledge and experience that would serve them well in the Confederate army service that was on the horizon.

Wright's interest in books and literature began to grow, and he became a collector of books, no small achievement given that the fact that books in Jackson County were few and far between, and many of the citizens of Jackson County had never learned to read. Therefore, Wright treasured his occasional trips to some of the larger towns in that part of the state, such as Victoria, the largest city and county seat of Victoria County, Texas. Wright would typically be sent to Victoria to secure goods for the Seven Up Ranch, that were not available in Texana. There existed at that time, two second-hand bookstores in Victoria that Wright loved to visit. The feeling that Wright was filled with, as he was about to enter the book shop, and as his steps neared the sanctified location, is one which only the true bibliophile can appreciate.

The two shops were very different from each other. The first was in the basement of one of the downtown brick buildings around the town square. This shop had a crypt-like atmosphere, with small windows that only very dimly lit the place. The wonderful mustiness that bookstores exhibit, was certainly present at this first store. Our learned medical brethren have said that there is a reason we associate certain odors with pleasurable past experiences: the olfactory senses of the brain are the most sensitive of all the sense organs of the human body, regarding recollecting happy memories. The owner of the first shop was a man who sat at a table beside the entry door, nearly hidden behind stacks and stacks of books yet to be placed on the shelves, or in some cases, to be shipped out. He was very quiet and quite monosyllabic in his communications, and Wright was never able to learn what his name was or anything about him. Wright always seemed to be the only customer present, and this led him to wonder how the man made a living at this vocation.

The other book shop in Victoria visited by Wright was a stark contrast with the first: it was on the ground floor, and decidedly better lit. This shop had an over-all wider selection of titles and subjects. The books were organized into sections such as historical works, poetry, science, philosophy, and so forth. Wright knew exactly where his favorite sections of the store were to be found, and glorious was the day when a new title in his favorite section appeared on the shelf.

Wright considered some of his books, his favorite ones, as almost sacred. Wright remembered, with a secret pride, where and when he had acquired each treasured volume, sometimes even how much money had given for them, and even recalled the peculiar details about them. For instance, many if not all of them would have a former owner's name written, in a beautiful hand, on the flyleaf. These names Wright could often recall.

Often, the former owner would add an inscription, such as when the book had been given as a gift at Christmas, and often that would include the geographical location of the owner. Some were from other states, far away, and this furthered the mystery of how this volume managed to get to Texas? Some of the volumes he acquired were printed more than a hundred years ago, yet such marvels were the book publishers of that day, that the books retained their shape and condition and still had a good spine and tight boards, even after the passage of a long spell of time. Surely their previous owner treasured it as much as Wright and took especial care to keep the book in a proper bookcase and away from any extreme heat, cold, and from water or wetness, which are the ever-certain destroyers of books. Wright would often look at the names of the former owners, usually written in beautiful penmanship, and wonder who he or she was? A hero or a rogue? An heiress or a poor peasant girl? Who knew? And why did this volume (he picked up an 8vo of the *Lay of the Last Minstrel*) come to be in the book shop for Wright to come across? Did some family member of the deceased owner fail to appreciate the fineness of the gold lettering on the cover? Perhaps the family member had no space on his bookshelves for it. Perhaps the impecunious family member had to sell it for to feed themselves? No — surely, thought Wright, the owner of such a lovely book as this would never allow themselves to fall into impecunious circumstances. An unexpected illness! That was it! And the dire circumstances forced the unfortunate family member to have to make the hard decision--that medicines and doctors come before books. Nothing could compel Wright to part with such a book as this … (he returned the book to its place on his shelf). In any event Wright would take his temporary custodianship of these volumes seriously, and who knows what the future would hold? Perhaps someone else would someday treasure these volumes after he was done with them … but that would be a very long time from now, he thought. On some volumes, the ones most cherished by Wright, would he feel compelled to write his own name in beautiful script: N. W. Wiseman ~ Texana, Texas. And sometimes: N. W. Wiseman ~ Carancahua Creek, Texas. Would someday some one wonder who he was, and how this volume came to be separated from him? Wright loved to look upon the fine gilt lettering on the spine and outer boards of the book cover. The strong spine and the solid feel of a true work of the printer's art. Even the smell of the volume, (as Wright opened the book and pressed his nose on to the pages, and sniffed) the unique, wonderful, slightly musty smell of an old book was delightful to him.

Thus, it was that the bricklayer and ranch hand was determined to make up for his lack of knowledge of literature, both because he was becoming fascinated with the English classics — and also so that he could understand Kate when she would talk about her favorite authors and poets. She knew all sorts of valuable literary information and possessed knowledge of such strange (to Wright) sounding terms, like for instance the ever-mysterious phrase *"iambic pentameter."* Kate would patiently explain about rhyme and meter and all sorts of novel ideas and literary concepts.

or The Maid of Saragoza

Wright was partial to the ever-popular Scott, and wished Kate shared his admiration for the Scottish author. Kate took issue with Wright's judgment, asserting that "Dickens is superior to Scott, in that he expresses the aspirations and hopes of the downtrodden and the disparity between the classes, and the hope that there will be an eventual leveling of the classes."

" Oh, so you are a leveler now?"

" A what?"

"A leveler, you know, a person favoring the removal of political, social, or economic inequalities."

"Silly goose! Dickens is more alive to great ideas."

"Well," said Wright, "in Scott's novels you have the most interesting scenes in history being played out amongst fascinating stories. His stories frequently involve the little fellow striving to win the day against his more powerful, stronger adversary."

"What on earth are you trying to say, silly goose?" said Kate.

" I mean Scotland striving to maintain its clans, its customs, its manners, in the face of a great and powerful invader, England … not a bad theme, I think," said Wright.

Kate looked askance at Wright and just smiled.

Again, Wright attempted to persuade her: "Take for instance, Bonnie Prince Charlie and his Jacobite's, denied the throne and defeated in war, were shown no quarter at Culloden by the English, and the rebels and their clans who did survive, were forbidden to associate together and to wear the tartan or play the pipes? Or the struggle of the Saxons against the cruel tyranny of their Norman Overlords in Ivanhoe?"

"Nevertheless, Dickens is superior to Scott," insisted Kate.

The young couple made their plans to start their life together. Wright had promised Kate he would obey her expressed wishes and become a teacher, and he and Kate would remove to some university town, and Wright would abandon his former vocations of bricklayer, house contractor and ranch hand. Kate made it plain to Wright that they would raise their family in some metropolis where there existed a great university and seat of learning, where Kate and Wright would discuss literature and all its associated themes, with their exalted colleagues and fellow professors of belles-lettres. The young couple had discussed becoming engaged, and Wright had begun to save up money.

But all this was not to be.

The election of Abraham Lincoln had put into motion a series of events which would change Jackson County forever. This event produced a growing movement across all the South. In Texana, a large and enthusiastic public meeting was held, and the Lone Star flag was unfurled. There was a parade, and a night procession with "transparencies," whose slogans painted on glass were illuminated by candles or kerosene lamps. Carried high on poles, they were clearly visible and easily read by the sidewalk throng. Leading the parade was the Lone Star flag made by the ladies of Texana and presented for the occasion. It was saluted by enthusiastic greetings of applause.

Next came the band, with stirring martial music, then the transparencies. The wording on the transparencies were: The Time Has Come! — States Rights — The Lone Star — Room for 15 — The Issue Is Upon Us — Voice of the People — Jackson County is Ready — Union Only With Honor — Who is Not for Us is Against Us — All Welcome to our Ranks — The First 30 — The 2nd of March — Revolutions Never Go Backwards — Cotton Is King — Crocketts and Bowies Not all Dead — None But Slaves Submit — No Room in Abe's Bosom for Us — Texas Is Sovereign — The Alamo — The North has Broken the Symbols of Union — Goliad and Gonzales, 1835 — Storming of Bexar — No Submission — We are with South Carolina.

That autumn of 1860, Wright's world seemed to disintegrate. That August, Kate had broken off their engagement, writing from her school: "I love you devotedly as you well know, and will be true to you always, but I do not like this binding promise. ... I think it best to test it."

And months later, he received the last letter from Kate. It began: "I just wanted to let you know personally that I plan to be married to. ..." The rest of the letter proceeded to explain about how she planned to become the bride of Edward Forbes, the son of a prominent railroad magnate, (and friend to no less a person than the newly elected president, Abraham Lincoln), and how they were going to set themselves up in the North, at said university town.

Later, upon the outbreak of hostilities, young Forbes, her husband, would secure an army commission as an engineer, with the rank of Brevet-Brigadier General in the Engineering Corps, and would have the responsibilities of supervising the construction and maintenance of the railroads used by the Federals to conduct the war to subjugate the South.

The last conversation Wright and Kate ever had occurred after Lincoln's election, when Wright happened to be passing Kate's parent's house, and Kate was sitting on the front porch. Kate had returned for one last visit with her family. She seemed to Wright to almost be a different person than the girl he had fallen in love with. After exchanging some reminiscing, Wright changed the subject to the current crisis:

or The Maid of Saragoza

"What will you do if Texas secedes?"

"I will stand by the good old Union, of course," was Kate's reply.

"And what will you do, Wright?" she asked, looking into his eyes for the first time that day.

"I go with Texas to the last, of course," he said.

"You will never win," she countered sarcastically, "the Northern states have superior armies and munitions of war. Your armies — a generous name for your armed rabble — will be crushed in one battle."

"We will never submit to being dictated to by the Republicans and abolitionists," he said.

"Then, the road into Texas will be soaked in Texas blood," she countered.

"But" said Wright, his love for his adopted State now taking over, said: "it will be intermixed with some of our enemies' blood, I think."

This awkward *tete-a-tete* ended their last conversation.

The question of whether Texas would remain in the Union was submitted to the people of the State. The answer was one of clear resolve: Texans voted three to one to leave the Union, on February the 23rd, 1861.

Chapter Nine

The soul hereafter will delight,
In all that pleased its earthly sight,
Will linger o'er each long-loved spot--
The sylvan glade, the rural grot,
The mountain-haunt, the winding shore
And all where bliss it found before.
— WRITTEN BY THE GRAVE OF AN INFANT

Before the young men of Jackson County marched off to war, there was just enough time for one last antiquarian excursion into the rural countryside, and this time the Old Sea Captain, John Billups, promised to show Wright some Indian Mounds along the West Carancahua.

"Today I will show you some of the works of the ancient Mound Builders. Now mount up and follow me," said the Sea Captain with a smile on his face. It was an undeniable fact that, in the several short years since Captain Billups had forsworn from any sea adventures, he had evinced a great interest in the natural world that existed in the streams, fields and forests of Jackson County. To some observers, it appeared that the old Captain's long tenure at sea, during his young manhood, had only served to increase his desire, in his middle age, to learn all he could about the wonders of terra firma.

Accompanying them was an individual who appeared to be about the same age as Wright but acting in a very singular manner. He was Davey Burnett and was dressed in the plain coarse suit of jeans that was typically worn by ranch hands. His stature was affected by a severe curvature of the spine, giving him a "hunchback" aspect. He wore a smile on his face most of the time, and was mute, although not deaf. He had experienced the traumatic event of the deaths of his family members in fire in which he alone had been awoken and dragged out of the burning home by the family dog, a large wolfhound. This had occurred when he was only a young child, but such are the workings of the human mind, that extreme trauma results in a mental disorder, and he never again spoke a word. That he was capable of hearing was borne out by the fact that he frequently and with zest requested that others sing to him his favorite songs. He had devised a system of communication with his hands to communicate these requests for music. He also was quite capable of jotting down the lyrics to a song that struck his fancy, and his pockets were often stuffed with pieces of paper evincing this.

"Mind if Davey goes along?" asked Wright, while Davey was walking by himself, off to the side of where the two men were conversing, oblivious and smiling and mimicking the actions of a person singing a song, yet no words, no sound, emitted from his lips.

"Davey Do-little they call him, from what I have seen, more like Davey Do-Nothing. Well, I suppose that is fine," answered Billups.

Davey made some motions with his hands to Wright, evidently a request for the *'Rose of Alabamy'*, and Wright sang:

> Away from Mississippi's vale,
> With my ol' hat there for a sail,
> I crossed upon a cotton bale,
> To Rose of Alabamy.
> Oh, brown Rosie,
> Rose of Alabamy.
> A sweet tobacco posey
> Is my Rose of Alabamy.
> A sweet tobacco posey
> Is my Rose of Alabamy.

On leaving their horses, the men climbed down from the gentle declivity that led to the lower flood plain which contained the *tumuli*. The West Carancahua had very little water in it at the time of the year. The most exquisite wildflowers of every description were in bloom along its banks. A variety of butterflies were gliding from flower to flower, sipping the nectar that each presented.

"Here is a Common Buckeye, or *Junonia coenia*. See the sets of eyes on his wings?" said the Captain, as he pointed out an uncommonly beautiful butterfly with wings brown and yellow and blue circles that seemed to have an iridescent blue, suggestive of the heavens above.

" The blue spots on the wings imitate a set of eyes, and acts to ward off predators. And, if the predator takes a bite at the "false" head, the butterfly only loses a chunk out of his wings, which he can survive, since the attack at the 'eyes' have spared the vital organs."

"And what is this large butterfly over here?" asked Wright.

"Ah, that is the Monarch, or *Danaus plexippus*. Truly, the King of Butterflies. They migrate south for the winter," replied Captain Billups.

"And this one that resembles a Monarch but is somewhat smaller?"

"Yes, that is a Painted Lady, *Vanessa cardui*. You see the difference in size?"

The Captain went on to describe in detail the favorite host plants and trees of each species of butterfly.

"You see each type of butterfly has a different host plant that is used to attach its eggs to, and then the caterpillars eat the plant. With Red Admirals, (or *Vanessa atalanta*, as old Linnaeus would say), it is the nettle plant, for instance."

The old Sea Captain mused as he walked along, inspired by watching the butterflies: "They are like winged blossoms," he thought, "and will the other flowers, will they too soar and take flight? Birds have nests, but the butterfly is Nature's freeman, free to stray to seek his food on every blossomed spray. The garden one wide banquet, the butterfly the daintiest reveler of the joyous earth! One drop of honey gives satiety, a second draught would drug thee past all mirth! Thy calm eyes never close. Yet, the soul of man upon thy wings forever soars in aspiration, thou his emblem of the new career that springs when death's arrest bids all his spirit bow. Mankind seeks his hope in thee of Immortality! Most gentle, most noble creature!"

Billups's reverie came to an end, and his mind returned to the present, and his companions.

The travelers walked along the flood plain as Captain Billups was pointing out the ancient burial mounds still extant and the wildflowers which grew upon them. They halted while Captain Billups was giving a disquisition on the fondness of Red Admirals for the tree sap of Ash trees, when the little party heard some thrashing sounds emanating from some of the brush that grew along the banks.

The Sea Captain interrupted his lesson on Lepidoptera, and said, in recounting his early experiences in Jackson County: "You hear something rustling? When I heard a rustling in the bushes, I knew it meant one of three things, an Indian, bear or a Methodist Circuit Rider, for while the first two mentioned were the far more numerous, the latter was far more active."

The suspense was broken when old Joe, the Owen's comical servant, emerged from the brush, where he had been hunting woodcocks.

"Well Joe, we thought you were a bear. Having any luck?"

" G'day gen'elmen, a mahty fine day it tis. So fah de woodcocks is winnin' de battle. Where are you gen'elmen heading?"

"I am showing some Indian Mounds to these young men, you are welcome to join us," said the Sea Captain.

or The Maid of Saragoza

As the party walked along a deer trail beside the riverbank, Joe saw a bevy of doves land at the edge of the shallow water in the river, then fly away, then return, then fly away again.

"Dem doves is trying to warn us," said Joe, with a concerned expression on his face. The remainder of the men smiled at this comment, illustrating, they thought, some of the superstitious beliefs of the Negroes.

A distant clap of thunder was heard, followed by another sound of thunder, and followed by another, each boom louder than the last. The day had gradually become hot and more humid, and there was a stillness to the air that seemed unnatural considering the distant darkening western sky. "God's mighty artillery" was announcing the coming of a storm.

"Captain, we may have to call a halt to our little excursion on account of the approaching storm. I'll lead us back to the horses," said Wright.

As Wright led the men back to the horses, a wave of wind suddenly hit the men, picking up the dead leaves and dust and scattering them into the air. The surrounding trees were now violently swaying back and forth in a rocking fashion.

The clouds were large and billowy and seemed to be almost boiling as the thunder sounded closer and closer. The dark gray clouds presented a most ominous meaning to the men. All of them had, by long experience as ranchers and farmers, learned to recognize the approach of a dangerous storm.

"The pilot," said Captain Billups, "in calm weather, will let a sea-boy trifle with the rudder, but, by my soul, when the winds howl, and waves arise, he stands by the helm himself! We will never make it back to the horses before this storm hits, I suggest we take shelter in that little alcove," as he spied a rock outcropping along the river. One opening seemed to be larger than the others, and Billups made for that opening.

"Oh no," said Joe, "ah nevuh have gone in dat cave. Dats de witches' cave. But if you gen'elmen all go, ah be glad t' 'company you."

"We have not time to debate that," shouted Billups, as the hail began to fall from the sky, striking the men and stripping the leaves from the trees, which despite their large size, were being whipped around in the wind gusts as if they were miniature playthings in the hand of a child.

The men walked into the opening sheltered by the grotto, their eyes becoming adjusted to the dim light. They could see a large caldron simmering over an open fire and many domestic articles were in sight, along with vegetable matter and bottles of power and other ingredients obviously used by the inhabitant of the cave. All this convinced the men, or at least convinced Captain Billups, that they were in fact in what was known as the Witches' Grot, a place much to be avoided under normal circumstances.

The old Sea Captain whispered as an aside to his comrades: "We are no doubt in the Witches' Grot, a place where witches and devils and other mischief-making beings are about on their errands; particularly those aerial people, the fairies. Those caverns in the rock outcropping we saw are said to be the favorite haunt of the fairies. Thank God it is not Halloween. …"

"Surely you don't believe …" but before Wright could finish his sentence, the figure of a female gradually became visible, as she walked toward the boiling cauldron.

It was the Negro Seer, Flora, who was dressed in a bright, vibrant colored dress, had her hair in a turban, and appeared to be in the midst of some incantation.

"Why have you come to my lodgings?" was all she said as she looked up from her concatenations and spell-making.

"Pardon the interruption, madam, (with a bow), I was showing some of the natural wonders and ancient fortifications of this valley to these young gentlemen, when we were forced to take cover in your domain from the storm outside," said Billups.

"I know what you are wondering, you are curious about my workshop, about my visions of the future. Yet I can see doubt in some of your faces," said the turbaned Sibyl.

"Your talent and powers are well known," said the Captain.

"As your fairness and breadth of mind, Captain Billups, are known to me," replied the harpy.

"Approach, then, Youth, and let me lay my hand upon your forehead," said Flora. She placed her hand on Wright's forehead as he approached. She shut her eyes and remained silent for a minute.

"Yes, I see a great many things. First, I see a terrible army poised to strike this land, and strangling it by blocking its ports and inlets," she said.

"Next, I see the role you will play in throwing off the yoke of the Oppressor. You will play a part in this, you and the other young men."

Wright could not resist the opportunity to ask a question that all young people are curious about.

"And please ma'am, do you see in your visions the face of the one I am to wed? And what is her name?" asked Wright.

The expression of the Sibyl changed to a pained expression, and after a moment of silence, all she said was: " I … I cannot see, there is a fog descending now over the picture."

The Sea Captain bowed gracefully, backed out and re-traced his steps towards the entrance to the cavern, saying, "come, gentlemen, we have taxed this lady enough for her visions of the future. Let us leave Miss Flora to her work, now that the storm has no doubt subsided. Madame, by your leave."

The four men left the Witches' Grot and felt rather relieved to have done so and suffered no harm for it. They were at a loss to understand just what the Sibyl was referring to during her declamation, as they resumed their trek back to their horses.

Chapter Ten

Draw near my gallant comrades and
A story to you I'll sing,
A sad and mournful song of war,
Tears to your eyes will bring.
One April morn on Shiloh's plains the
Rising sun displayed,
One hundred thousand soldiers in
Battle line arrayed.

— SHILOH'S HILLS

"The Texana Guards" had been formed as the local militia unit for Jackson County, even before the war clouds gathered on the horizon. Colonel Clark Owen had been instrumental in founding this organization. Initially, Clark Owen had not been a secessionist, but like many Texans, he reached a point where it became evident that the Northern leaders were determined to enlarge and centralize power in the Federal government, reduce the autonomy of the States, and dominate the South economically and politically.

Eventually, most Texans, many of them at one time opposed to secession, overwhelmingly supported leaving the Union, even before the firing on Fort Sumter. In May of 1861, most of the boys along the two Carancahuas had been drilling with the Texana Guards. In June of that year ex-governor Stockdale stood on the steps of the courthouse in Texana, to deliver a speech encouraging the young men of Jackson County to join the companies then being formed, to be eventually admitted into the Southern Confederacy. The new volunteers brought whatever firearms they had available, which included all manner of firearms. Some even brought the antique flintlock guns their grandfathers had used in the last rebellion, in 1776.

When the Texans reported for duty, the truth was, that many of them had no guns at all, others had unreliable weapons, and some with the old flintlocks. Many of the guns had no locks or firing mechanisms. Most of them were manufactured between 1805 and 1815. Others believed some of the weapons dated back to Miles Standish. There were squirrel rifles of every age, style, and bore. Shotguns, single-barreled, double-barreled, old and new, flintlock, percussion, or no lock at all. Carbines of every character, pistols of every patent, and huge knives that were considered too little

or The Maid of Saragoza

to be useful if they were less than two pounds.

The Texans were having to learn to do without many of the staples of ordinary life. With the war came the Federal blockade of the Texas coastline. Occasionally there were blockade runners that were able to break through, such as the time General Albert Sidney Johnston was able to secure thousands of excellent Enfield rifles from England. But it was clear to the Texans that the fledgling Confederate government would have to rely on the Southern people's ability to improvise, in training, equipping, and arming, it's soldiers.

A character trait, or one might almost call it a racial characteristic, of Americans, and of Southerners in particular, has always been their ability to work best under pressure. Hopelessness and despair do not come readily to such a breed. Thus, it was that the Texans, cutoff by the blockade, from their customary supplies, both militarily and civilian, armed themselves and prepared and carried out WAR ... through improvisation, substitution, and the iron will of her people.

The young men of Jackson County began to drill and to learn the school of the soldier in the "camps of instruction" at Houston and Galveston. The boys along the two Carancahuas who would become soldiers all had known each other well. Some of these were Wright Wiseman and his older brother William, William Stayton and his brother James, Samuel Dutart, W. B. McDowell and his brother Eugene, and John Bolling.

Wright and William Wiseman were accompanied by their body-servant, Ben, who was about the same age and with whom they experienced the joys, and occasional sorrows, of growing up. Wright was greatly attached to Ben and was solicitous of him in every respect. Ben was a loyal friend as well, and assisted Wright in carrying out his chores and responsibilities on the Ranch. Ben shared in his entertainments such as hunting and fishing. It was a relationship which transcended that of master and slave, and it was a relationship which the Yankee could never understand. It was also a relationship which the Yankee sought later to deny, deride and erase from the history books.

Of all these volunteers, the most flamboyant was William Stayton, who lived just south of the 7-Up Ranch, at his family's plantation, Stayton Hall. He was a hell-for-leather type of aristocrat, who prided himself in possessing the finest liquors, riding the fastest horse, and carrying off the most rings in the Ring Tournaments. He was as extreme a secessionist as he was with every other facet of his life, promising to "fly the black flag," to "give no quarter," and that the only way to win independence was "to kill every Yankee that fell into his hands." In terms of his educational pursuits, his interests were those other than the kind found in books, and he was very indifferent about his reading and writing.

W. B. McDowell and his brother were good, solid stock raisers and minders, used to providing for oneself on the cattle drives, and living in the out-of-doors, and more interested in the science of breeding good cattle and horses, than chasing after the gentler sex.

John Bolling was a tall, quiet, thoughtful boy that had acquired a modest amount of book-learning, as well as working the family ranch, located at the confluence of the two Carancahuas.

There were also three volunteers that, due to their peculiarities, and physical limitations, caused some concern with the Confederate authorities: Davey Burnett, the stoop-shouldered mute boy, was nevertheless adamant about becoming a member of the company being formed by Clark Owen. The Confederate officials, however, had refused to accept him on the ground that he was physically unfit for duty as a soldier.

To cheer Davey up, Wright Wiseman would suggest to his friend Stayton:

"Davey is a bit blue. The Confederate army refuses to accept him. Could you cheer him up with a few lines of *Maryland*?" said Wright.

Stayton said for the benefit of the others present: "Ever since Davey heard me sing Randall's lyrics about the State in which I was born, he has been requesting it:

> The despot's heel is on the shore,
> Maryland, my Maryland!
> His torch is at thy temple door
> Maryland, my Maryland!
> Avenge the patriotic gore,
> That flecked the streets of Baltimore!
> And be the battle queen of yore,
> Maryland, my Maryland!"

Davey's face lit up and he bobbed his crooked form up and down, as would an excited child, when he heard these words sung in a strong, clear voice by the mercurial William Stayton.

Frank Burwell, known to all as "Frankie," was a very rotund, convivial young man who was also known to have never declined a meal or food of any kind. He weighed almost three hundred pounds and was only accepted into the service when several other volunteers refused to join unless Frankie was accepted. Grudgingly, the army relented, as will be explained below, and Frankie was admitted. "Zounds!" was his favorite expression. Somehow, he had never shed his corpulence despite his campaigning regimen. "Zounds!" he would exclaim at supper time, "How do the Generals expect us to maintain our strength on these meager portions?"

Maurice Simons was the third volunteer who had a physical impediment and came from a family well known and well-respected to all the denizens in and around Texana. He volunteered to be the commissary cook and was one-legged. He had lost his leg in the Mexican War, where he had been shot by a Mexican soldier, and then in turn killed his assailant. His leg had been taken off with a meat cleaver in the field without the benefit of any chloroform. He was given very little chance of survival, and that little chance disappeared when yellow fever broke out in his hospital ward. He somehow, against all odds, survived to return home to Texas. Simons was likewise initially rejected by Confederate authorities, due to his lameness. However, the army again was forced to relent due to protests from the other Texans, and he entered the Provisional Confederate States Army as a second lieutenant and eventually a Major in the Brigade Commissary.

William P. Rogers, an eminent Houston lawyer, had the rank of lieutenant-colonel, and was also a veteran of the Mexican War. When he first saw, Maurice Simons, at the Camp of Instruction, Simons was on horseback.

"I say, sir, did you have a brother in the army in Mexico?" asked Rogers.

Maurice squinted, and before he could answer, Rogers continued: "I believe I served with your brother in the Mexican war, I can see the resemblance. He was our cook. He had been shot in the leg, and he killed the Mexican soldier who shot him. His leg had to be removed in the field, and he later died."

"I am that man," said Simons.

"No, that man died," said Rogers.

Major Simons then rode the horse around to the other side of Rogers to show his missing leg.

"By G__, it is you!" exclaimed Rogers.

After the Texas volunteers refused to serve unless Davey Burnett, Frankie Burwell and Maurice Simons were all admitted to the regiment, the Confederate officials relented, and the three "nonconformists" could join their fellows in the regiment.

In October of 1861, Colonel John C. Moore was commissioned Colonel of the Second Texas Infantry Regiment, in the Provisional Army of the Confederate States of America. The regiment consisted of one company from each of the following counties: Jackson, Brazos, Burleson, Gonzales, Lee, Robertson, Chambers, Harris (multiple companies) and one from Galveston.

The regiment received the designation "Second" Texas due to the fact that influential Senator Wigfall of Texas had secured for another regiment that of "First" Texas and the First was sent to Virginia. The Second Texas was assigned to fight in the western parts of the Confederacy, (meaning initially in Tennessee and Mississippi), and if ever attacked, in Texas itself.

The Second Texas missed the earlier battles in the west, including the disastrous battle at Fort Donelson, which took place in frigid February 1862, and in which about 15,000 Confederate troops were surrendered. These 15,000 troops thus were removed from use by the Confederates at the very time their numbers would perhaps have turned the tide of the battle at Shiloh, in April of 1862. At the time of that battle, the Confederacy had been pushed back nearly 400 miles to a point where Nashville was abandoned, and the State of Tennessee was essentially lost to the Confederacy.

It was known to the Federals that the Confederates were heavily fortifying at Corinth, Mississippi. Corinth was in northern Mississippi, at an important crossroads of two Southern railroad lines. The prospects for the Confederates now were looking very dreary in the West, and the commander, Albert Sidney Johnston, was under great pressure to turn the fortunes around.

General Albert Sidney Johnston was considered a gallant military hero in the finest traditions of the Old South. Born in Kentucky and having graduated from the Military Academy at West Point, he immigrated to Texas during the 1836 Revolution. He served in the Mexican War of 1846-48. He had also been appointed, during the 1850's, as Colonel of the 2nd (U. S.) Cavalry Regiment stationed in Texas, that famous unit, which was destined to give, to both North and South, so many generals of renown in the War Between the States.

General Johnston appeared the very picture of Mars. He wore his hair long in the fashion of the times and had a dark moustache. His stature was that of a giant, and the soldiers could not but look upon him in awe when they saw him in the magnificent array of the resplendent dress uniform of a full Confederate General officer. He was no less impressive when he sat his mighty steed, a tall Thoroughbred Bay, named "Fire-eater".

Lately, after the fall of Forts Donelson and Henry, General Johnston had come under extreme scrutiny. Taciturn of speech, and quiet by nature, he refused to fight back against the calumnies spread by the jealous and envious. He would only say: "The test of merit in my profession with the people is success. It is a hard rule, but I think it right." However, the people's patience was already nearing an end. He, and the Confederacy, needed a big victory in the West. President Davis, already a close friend and supporter, never lost faith in him, and believed him the best general in the Confederacy.

It was assumed by all familiar with the war, that the next great battle of the war in the West would be fought at Corinth, Mississippi. The Confederates were concentrating their troops there, and General P.G.T. Beauregard was ringing the town with cannon and fortifications. Yet fate was to intervene, and instead, an obscure location on a bluff above the Tennessee River, about twenty miles north of Corinth, would be the location of the Great Battle of the West.

General Grant had instructed General Sherman, his subaltern, to choose a base on the Tennessee River, from which to organize and drill his army that was to attack the Confederates at Corinth and end the war. The invasion of the lower South had begun in the early months of 1862. Sherman had chosen a campground, for his base of operations, out of a practical wilderness, on the Tennessee river, a place consisting of heavy timber interspersed by a few humble cabins and tiny sharecropper farms, near an obscure river-landing called Pittsburg Landing. The battle that was to take place here became better known by the name of the church that was on the battleground: Shiloh Church. This location was thinly peopled and heavily forested. The Federal campground was on high, broad and dry ground, with the Tennessee River at their back and two creeks (Owl Creek and Lick Creek) on either flank. The position was a strongly defensive position, protected on both flanks by creeks and the rear by the River. Grant and Sherman committed the cardinal sin, however, of failing to fortify the camp. This was not necessarily common at this stage in the war, although experience would show that it should have been done. Grant and Sherman were still learning the hard lessons in Generalship.

Grant and Sherman were waiting to affect a juncture with General Buell's army, which was marching west towards Pittsburg Landing to join up with Grant and Sherman. General Johnston knew that time was of the essence and was furiously bringing together various scattered elements of his army, to try and surprise the unsuspecting Federals. Eventually, at the end of March 1862, General Johnston had collected about 44,000 troops and reorganized the army into separate corps: one each for Generals Hardee, Bragg and Polk, with a "reserve" corps under Breckinridge. General Beauregard was second in command and was given the task of devising the actual plan of operations by General Johnston.

When General Van Dorn had taken his army in February and marched for Arkansas, it was intended that he would be present, back in Tennessee, for General Albert Sidney Johnston's surprise attack on the invading Yankees coming down the Tennessee River. Van Dorn and General Dabney Maury had previously met with General Johnston at Corinth. In discussing the upcoming battle, General Van Dorn said to Johnston:

"General, I met upon the river a fine Texas regiment, the Second Texas, Colonel John C. Moore commanding. I ordered it to come at once to you for this impending battle. Please remember that it is to be one of the regiments of the brigade I am going to make up for General Maury."

"I will remember," replied General Johnston, "but I wish you would leave Maury with me now, and I could at once make up a good brigade for him." However, Van Dorn could not do without Maury, and thus, because Van Dorn's army had not returned from fighting at the Battle of Elkhorn Tavern, Van Dorn and Maury and their men missed the Battle of Shiloh.

To make the surprise attack on Grant and Sherman, the army would march the twenty-three miles to Pittsburg Landing along three different roads. Although Grant and Sherman knew the Confederates were nearby, they were absolutely convinced that no offensive operations would be attempted by the Rebels, and that the Confederates would dig-in behind their fortifications at Corinth and wait for the Federals to attack.

The weather in early April of 1862 was very wet, causing the approach to Pittsburg Landing to be slow. It was with great difficulty that the artillery was hauled over the mud roads. The hoped-for attack date of April 5 had to be revised, and Sunday, April 6 ended up the day of ordeal.

General Johnston, before leaving his headquarters, the "Rose Cottage" of Mrs. Inge in Corinth, had ordered 500 metal caskets to be delivered to Corinth. Little did he suspect that after the battle, one of them would be used to transport his own body back to New Orleans for burial!

Mrs. Inge remembered how the General's blue eyes gleamed as he prepared to ride away. When she asked the General if she might fix him a couple of sandwiches and some cake, he politely refused saying: "No, thank you, Mrs. Inge, we soldier's travel light." Unbeknownst to the General, she slipped two sandwiches and some cake into his coat pocket

or The Maid of Saragoza

before he rode off.

General Johnston was, as previously mentioned, quiet and slow of speech, which was mistaken by some as indecisiveness. In truth, in matters of deliberation, he was a man of intense thought and preferred to remain passive during critical discussions, wishing to hear other's viewpoints. He had led a truly exemplary life, having experienced and overcame financial reverses, and the death of his first wife. Yet he emerged with his integrity intact.

Due to the wet, muddy roads and the greenness of the troops, during the approach to the Federal camps, there was hesitation on the part of General Beauregard. About 5 o'clock in the afternoon of April 5, there was a conference with all the generals present. Beauregard, who had up to now been adamant about the need to strike Grant with alacrity, suddenly lost his nerve. It was Beauregard's contention, now, that the noise made by the inexperienced troops and the delay in forming the army for attack had served notice to the enemy who would be found "entrenched to the eyes" and ready for the attack. For all these reasons, Beauregard now urged that the attack be abandoned, and the army be returned to Corinth.

General Johnston was shocked at Beauregard's statements! He listened patiently to Polk, who said his troops were prepared and eager to fight. Breckinridge also reported to Johnston that his men had ample provisions.

After considering all the viewpoints, General Johnston said: "Gentlemen, we shall attack at daylight tomorrow," said General Johnston. As the conference broke up, General Johnston was heard to tell his aide, Colonel William Preston, (his close friend and brother of his first wife): "I would fight them (the enemy) if they were a million! They can present no greater front between these two creeks than we can; and the more they crowd in there, the worst we can make it for them."

To his aide Edward Munford he said with determination: "I have ordered a battle for tomorrow at daylight, and I intend to hammer 'em!"

The first line of enemy tents lay about the Shiloh Church, a log cabin church in the wilderness near Pittsburg Landing, and from which the battle took its name. When the Confederate army encamped the night of April 5, they were within two miles of Shiloh Church. Incredibly, the Federal army was in complete ignorance of how close this large army was to their campgrounds.

A few Yankees were looking for water to fill canteens, and had strayed into Confederate hands, out in the woods. They were brought to Confederate staff officers for questioning. As the Yank prisoners scanned the seeming endless line of Confederate troops in gray and butternut, they said, guilelessly: "This means a battle. They (gesturing toward the Federal camps) don't expect anything of this kind back yonder."

General Johnston's original concept was an attack with corps abreast, each corps being assigned a sector of the front. However, Beauregard's revision called for an attack by succeeding waves of infantry, with each corps aligned one behind the other, across the entire front. The basic premise was that no force the enemy could amass could cut through three double lines of Confederates. General Johnston accepted this modification of Beauregard. The conference the night before the battle also resulted in Johnston's tactical plan to turn the enemy's left flank to cut off his line of retreat to the Tennessee River, and throw him back on Owl Creek, where he would be obliged to surrender. The night before the battle, the soldiers were read General Johnston's battle order, which concluded thusly: "…with the trust that God is with us your Generals will lead you confidently to the combat, assured of success." The army, Johnston proclaimed, would be fighting with "the eyes and hopes of eight millions of people" resting upon them.

Chapter Eleven

In gardens you may note amid the dearth,
The crocus breaking earth,
And near the snowdrops tender white and green,
The violet in its screen.

But many gleams and shadows needs must pass,
Along the budding grass,
And weeks go by, before the enamored South,
Shall kiss the rose's mouth.

— Timrod's *Spring*

General Johnston was sipping coffee, a drink he relished, when the sound of gunfire reached him as he huddled around his staff officers in the darkness, on that crisp Spring morning. Dawn was just about to break, and after a miserable cold, rainy night, the glorious "Sun of Austerlitz" was about to appear, warming and drying the soil about to be christened with the blood of the very Flower of Southern Chivalry.

"Gentlemen, there is the first gun, what is the time?" asked General Johnston calmly.

"5:14 a.m." said his aide, Edward Munford.

General Beauregard later described the Confederate advance on April 6th as "like an Alpine avalanche." The front line alone consisted of twenty-two regiments and two battalions of infantry divided into four brigades, in all over nine thousand troops.

General Johnston determined to lead the attack from the front. Beauregard was to remain in the rear, sending the reserves forward when needed. Johnston summoned his staff. He mounted his Thoroughbred Bay, "Fire-eater," exciting great admiration with his appearance as a horseman. Like an antique Cavalier, his face was "aflame with a fighting spirit." He was described as "the ideal embodiment of the fiery essence of war." Johnston then told his staff: "To-night we will water our horses in the Tennessee River."

Early reports now reached Johnston that the Federals had been completely caught off guard. General Johnston asked General Beauregard: "Can it be possible they are not aware of our presence?" Beauregard replied: "It is scarcely possible they are laying a trap for us."

Reflecting confidence, the commanding General rode up towards

Hardee's front line, in the vicinity of Seay field. Some Arkansas troops were encountering stiff resistance, and General Johnston sought to encourage the men, shouting: "Men of Arkansas! You Toothpick Men! They say you boast of your prowess with the Bowie knife. Today you wield a nobler weapon — the bayonet. Employ it well."

Upon receiving word that Bragg's line was hard pressed, Johnston rode over to the right. Upon riding through the camp of the 18th Wisconsin, Johnston observed a Confederate plundering a captured tent, and rebuked the plunderer, saying: "None of that, sir; we are not here for plunder!" Then seeing the disappointment on the soldier's face, Johnston picked up a little tin cup and said: "Let this be my share of the spoils today." Thenceforth, General Johnston carried the little tin cup in his hand as a "substitute" for his sword. On the Confederate right flank, nearest the River, was Brigadier General David Stuart's Federal brigade. It was reported (incorrectly) to Johnston that an entire Federal division was encamped here. Johnston accordingly ordered two brigades, Chalmer's and Jackson's, (having just advanced through Prentiss's camp, in the center of the line), to withdraw and move to the right, to attack the supposed brigade of Stuart.

The Second Texas, of which Company K was made up of the boys from Jackson County, formed a part of Jackson's brigade. General Johnston sought particularly to throw the Second Texas into the fight:

"Bring up that Texas Regiment!" shouted General Johnston.

" Here we are!" shouted back Captain Ashbel Smith.

The Texans had crossed Locust Grove branch and approached Stuart's brigade on the right. Ahead loomed the camps of the 71st Ohio and the 55th Illinois.

General Johnston shouted instructions: "Remember to fire low, fire at their belts."

The Second Texas had just arrived in Corinth on April 1st. The regiment had marched part way, and ridden steamboat's part way, during the long trek from Houston. On April 1st they were also given new uniforms. They were of white wool, there having been no time to color them. The jackets contained a nine-button front and a stand-up collar. They were like the type of garment typically worn by slaves on plantations. These white uniforms were not at all appreciated by the soldiers, as it occurred to them that wearing these white uniforms made them excellent targets in the woods, for the Yankees. Even worse, none of the uniforms had any sizes marked. What ensued on April 1st was a comical scene that resembled a Saturday afternoon horse-trading day in a country town. The men were parading around, some with trousers dragging under their heels, while others scarcely reached the tops of their socks.

Private Burwell, whose uniform was too small by far, gave him the ludicrous appearance of a stuffed toad.

"Zounds!" he exclaimed, "Do the generals expect us all to be killed, and want us to wear our burial shrouds?" Whereupon he proceeded to roll around in the brown dirt, to properly "initiate" his uniform.

Private William Stayton observed that he had no problem with the color of the uniform and had already purchased a white uniform of undyed cotton, en route from Texas to Corinth.

"The owner recently deceased?" asked one of the officers about his new purchase.

"Why yes, I think so."

"And that caused you no concern?" said the smiling officers.

"What …?" asked Stayton.

The officers laughed heartily at Stayton's naivete.

Now the Second Texas were initiating the new undyed uniforms as they approached the camp of the 55th Illinois. Upon first impression, it appeared the Federals had already fled the camp for the protection of the Yankee gunboats at Pittsburg Landing. However, it turned out there were some Yankees still skulking about in some old Negro cabins, waiting for their opportunity to ambush the Confederates.

It was at this point that General Albert Sidney Johnston personally ordered the Second Texas, commanded by his old friend, Colonel John C. Moore, to charge the camp and capture it.

Girardey's (Confederate) battery, who was posted on a hill to the rear, began shelling the Yankee camp, to aid the Texans. After a fierce fight, the Confederates had the remaining Yankees on the run. Unbeknownst at the time, there were no other Federal forces behind the fleeing troops and the objective, and the road was literally clear all the way to Pittsburg Landing. If only this knowledge could have been known, perhaps General Johnston's prediction about watering their horses in the Tennessee River would have been realized.

Meanwhile the Texans explored the veritable tent "city" the Yankees had erected in the wilderness, with "streets" laid out and crisscrossing at precise right angles, and each tent furnished with many of the comforts of "home", all of which the Yankees now had been forced to abandon. The food prepared by the Yankee cooks for Sunday morning was still simmering in various pots, although the mouths which were consuming the delicious breakfast, were not those intended by the cooks. While marching

or The Maid of Saragoza

prisoners to the rear, one of the Federal officers, trying to put on a brave face, struck up a conversation with his Confederate captors:

"You know you didn't surprise us. We knew of your presence and were ready for your attack."

Frankie Burwell, looking over the various fine meats and viands that were simmering on the flames, and taking in the elaborate breakfast delicacies, filling the air with pleasing aromas, was not convinced, and replied to the officer: "Zounds! If we have not surprised you, then I am willing to pronounce your cooks the most dedicated cooks in the history of warfare!"

The Texans hearing this gave out a hearty laugh.

The Second Texas was not the only regiment at Shiloh that was plagued by the color of their uniforms. The 18th Louisiana, Colonel Mouton's fine regiment, were dressed in blue uniforms, much like the enemy. They were fired upon by Confederate regiments and experienced serious casualties, all morning. They retaliated whenever they received a volley. The Louisianaian's had a sound military reason for their conduct, saying: "We fire at anybody what fires at us — G_d d__n."

The Second Texas had made several successful charges that morning, but their luck had run out. Crossing a muddy ploughed field, and, having lost contact with Colonel Moore, they were temporarily under the command of General Hardee and his staff officers. Hardee warned them not to fire on their friends in the woods in the distance. The Texans could clearly see the troops being referenced were not friends, and were in fact Federals, and that those Federals were opening fire. Facing a situation of either disobeying Hardee's order, or experiencing a sure death from the Federals in the woods ahead, they began to flee backwards, in a pell-mell fashion.

One of Hardee's officers withdrew his revolver and pointed it at the Texans: "Halt, cease firing I say, those are your friends you are firing into!" he shouted.

"Those are most certainly not our friends, old fellow, and we are getting out of this death trap you have led us into!" said William Stayton, as he fell back along with his fellow Texans.

"Cowards, halt I say, I will report you as cowards to General Hardee!"

"You may d--n well report us whatever you want, we will not stay on this field any longer!" replied Stayton, as he scurried out of harm's way with the other Texans.

The entire unfortunate situation was later used (and misused) by various factions, some wanting to impugn cowardice on the part of the

Second Texas, others wanting to vindicate the bravery of the regiment. The truth was that Hardee and his staff foolishly mistook the Federals for some of Breckinridge's men, and by failing to discover their mistake, caused many more needless casualties. This incident later had ramifications on the regiment at Corinth, with the Second Texas wanting to prove their sterling worth and bravery, against these unfounded accusations of cowardice by Hardee. To make matters worse, Clark Owen, the Captain of Company K, was killed in this unfortunate affair. General Johnston had known him in his earlier days in Texas, and he was much disturbed when he heard the news of his death.

By mid-day on the first day of the battle, the Confederates had pushed the Federals back toward the Tennessee River and the creeks, as planned by General Johnston. Many thousands of Federals fled in panic and were cowering at the river landing. Yet some of the Federals stubbornly fought back. It was by this time that Federal General Hurlbut, with about forty-five hundred men, held the peach orchard. Prentiss and about a thousand soldiers were also holding a sunken road that had been built into a very strong position, known to the participants as the "Hornet's Nest,"— a place of many whizzing minie balls. Prentiss had seven Federal batteries, about thirty-eight guns, along this defensive line. The trees and brush that surrounded these troops added to the strength of the Federal line.

The time was now about half past one o'clock in the afternoon. Breckinridge had been struggling unsuccessfully with Statham's, Bowen's and a portion of Stephens's command, who were engaged in a fight with Hurlbut's troops in the vicinity of the peach orchard. McArthur's Federal troops had moved to help Stuart's men against Chalmers. Two regiments from Jackson's brigade (19th Alabama and Second Texas) veered off to the right to help Chalmers.

General John C. Breckinridge was an impressive figure in his Confederate uniform. He had been Vice-President of the United States under Buchanan. Unlike most politician-generals in the War Between the States, who were dubious practitioners of the military art, Breckinridge was an able and talented leader. However, all his knowledge and experience had proved fruitless in the immediate problem he faced.

Breckinridge galloped over to General Johnston to explain his dilemma:

"General, I have a Tennessee regiment that won't fight."

Governor Isham Harris (who was the Confederate Governor of Tennessee and was one of General Johnston's volunteer aides), overhearing this, responded:

"General Breckinridge, show me that regiment."

"Let the Governor go to them," said General Johnston.

Governor Harris, with pistol in hand, with difficulty, prodded the Tennessee soldiers a bit, but ultimately had no more success than Breckinridge.

Meanwhile, General Johnston was attempting to organize a massive attack, in hopes of smashing the Federal position.

However, Governor Harris returned to Johnston and said he had no more success than Breckinridge, and a few minutes later, General Breckinridge returned and in an emotional voice, said to General Johnston:

"I cannot get them to make the charge."

"Oh yes, General, I think you can."

"I have tried and failed," said Breckinridge.

"Then I will help you," said General Johnston.

Riding "Fire-eater" to where the recalcitrant regiment was standing, Johnston had the tiny tin cup he had previously taken from the captured camp, in his hand. He touched the soldier's bayonets with the cup as he rode down the line, making a sound as he did so: tink … tink … tink. As he did this, he addressed the hesitant Tennesseans:

"Men, the enemy are stubborn; we must use the bayonet. I want you to show General Beauregard and General Bragg what you can do with your bayonets … soldiers, get ready."

He continued to ride down the line, tapping his little tin cup on their bayonets.

He further said to the men in line: "Soldiers, are you ready to drive the invaders of your country from our soil? Are you with me to defend your homes and hearths? Remember that your wives, your children, your sisters and your mothers are counting on you! Are you ready?"

"We are!" they shouted as if from one voice.

"I will lead you!" shouted the confident General, and as he did so, he wheeled about his thoroughbred bay, Fire-Eater, in a violent fashion, and began to ride determinedly toward the enemy line.

The entire line, from Stephens's brigade on the west, to Jackson's brigade on the east, perhaps 3,000 soldiers, trembled with irresistible ardor. It was about 2 o'clock in the afternoon when General Johnston stepped off and said:

"Charge forward. Common time march."

McArthur's Yankees were now visible in the ravine just ahead.

"Double quick march!" shouted Johnston.

The Yankees could not resist such an attack and were driven northward from the peach orchard. It was during this charge that General Johnston was hit in the leg, by a ball. He failed to realize the seriousness of the wound, in the excitement of the charge.

Thus wounded, he reeled in the saddle, and having been carried by staff officers to a nearby ravine, was laid down, and bled to death, having previously detached his physician, Doctor Yandell, to care for wounded Federals. Had the General not done this, his physician would only have had to apply a simple tourniquet.

During the battle, privates Sterling Fisher and Davey Burnett were sent to the rear to obtain water in canteens for the poor suffering soldiers who were scattered across the hills and hollows over which the charge had taken place. The sun of that April afternoon was warm, and many of the wounded were crying out for water.

One prostrated Federal, a Captain, his leg obviously mangled, let out a loud groan as Fisher and Burnett passed.

"Is there anything we can do for you?" asked the Texan.

"I would be grateful if you could straighten me out, as my leg is badly shot," he answered.

Another Federal lying near him asked: "Water, for G_d's sake, water!"

"Move me out of the sun!" asked a third Yankee.

The wounded Federal Captain then asked:

"These two men are members of my company. Would you be so good as to move them beside me so that we might assist each other?"

A bed of leaves was made, and Fisher and Burnett placed the two men beside the Captain, as requested.

Fisher noticed the Captain wore a heavy gold watch.

"I recommend that you put that watch in your pocket, lest you be robbed by a plunderer."

"I am sure I cannot recover and wish for you to keep it for your kindness."

"No, but I will put it in your pocket," Fisher answered.

Fisher and Burnett left several filled haversacks and some filled canteens by their sides.

Davey made a motion with his hands to Fisher, and moved his mouth as if trying to talk, however no words came out of his mouth. All that emitted from him was "ugh, ugh, ugh." Fisher, from prior experience, knew what Davey Burnett was trying to say.

"Davey these gentlemen do not need a song, they need some medical attention," said Fisher.

Undeterred, Davey continued to make gesticulations until Fisher smiled and relented:

"Very well, Davey, what do you want to hear? *'Dan Tucker'*?
Fisher began to sing:

> Old Dan Tucker was a fine old man,
> Washed his face with a fryin' pan,
> Combed his hair with a wagon wheel,
> And died with a toothache in his heel.
> Get out the way, Old Dan Tucker,
> You're too late to get your supper,
> Get out the way, Old Dan Tucker,
> You're too late to get your supper."

"Is that man simple?" asked one of the Federals.

"No, only eccentric. He is a lover of fine melodies. He is mute, but not deaf."

"Then by all means sing away," said the Yankee Captain, "anything to take our minds off our awful pain."

The three Federals were grateful and asked that Fisher write their names and regiments in a memorandum book. In returning the book, and on their reading the names with that of, "Second Texas Infantry," they looked at Fisher and Davey Burnett in astonishment.

"Are you really Texans?" they asked incredulously.

"Yes, why do you ask?"

"We have prayed not to fall into the hands of Texans, as we have been told we would be shown no quarter, and most certainly be butchered."

"Did we not fight you like men? And are not the brave always kind?" said Fisher.

They responded: "You fought us more like demons than men; but surely your kindness cannot be questioned."

The now grateful soldiers were Illinois troops, and the Texans hailed an ambulance and placed them in it.

Private Burwell managed to survive the two-day battle and was seen by many on the retreat to Corinth, on Monday. He was carrying, in addition to his accoutrements of war, an armload of treasure, courtesy of some unknown Federal officer who had brought some of the refinements of home, to his tent at Pittsburg Landing. Burwell had, among other things, a gilded French mirror, a box of good Havana cigars, two bottles of imported wine, and most curious of all, a pair of lady's silk stockings!

When the noble Albert Sidney Johnston was struck down on that first day of Shiloh, so evaporated the Confederate hopes of driving Grant into the Tennessee River. General Beauregard, who assumed command after Johnston was stricken, called off one last push across Dill branch while daylight remained on that Sunday first day battle of Shiloh. This was the crucial mistake that caused the battle to be ultimately lost. 9,000 Federal troops were at that moment cowering in fear at the docks at Pittsburg Landing. General Beauregard's rationale was that the battle had been won, and Grant would retreat in the night. Instead, General Buell and his army arrived Sunday night, and increased the combined Federal armies to 55,000 men. Consequently, on Monday April 7th the Confederates were pushed back and eventually retreated to Corinth.

Thus, the great battle of the West, that both sides believed would end the war, Shiloh, did no such thing. In fact, far from ending the war, Shiloh instead only showed that both sides were in deadly earnest, and that both sides would never give in, absent complete subjugation. The war would be measured, not in days, not in months, but in years.

The body of General Johnston was brought back to Mrs. Inge's house, where it was cleaned and dressed in a fresh uniform. Mrs. Inge found in his old uniform pockets some crumbs of the cakes she had slipped into his pocket the day he left Corinth. She carefully and lovingly clipped three locks of his hair. She sent one to Mrs. Johnston, one was placed in the cornerstone of the courthouse at Corinth, and one was to be placed in the cornerstone of the Confederate monument at Shiloh, after the war.

Major Garrett, whose duty it was to call the roll each morning, found the ranks of company K considerably thinned as a result of the great battle of Shiloh. He and Maurice Simons were discussing this subject on the road back to Corinth.

"Simons, those killed were George Baylor, Eugene McDowell, Jim Futhey, Captain Clark Owen, Gorman and Henry Myers. William McDowell and John Rogers have mortal wounds and will no doubt die," said Major Garrett.

"Yes, but the regiment covered itself with glory," reminded Simons, "In addition to the fights on Sunday, the regiment made two splendid charges on Monday. The regimental flag had six holes in it, including one in the staff. General Beauregard has authorized the word 'Shiloh' to be inscribed on our battle flag, and henceforth the regiment is to be called 'sharpshooters' and to be in the vanguard of the army."

"But...Clark Owen killed, an irreparable loss!" asked Simons as he shook his head.

or The Maid of Saragoza

"Yes, and it never should have happened," said Garrett.

"What do you mean?" asked Simons.

"He was about to escape that trap Hardee's men led us to, when his horse got bogged in a muddy ploughed field, and the brute just gave up. Five Yankees with their bayonets, were on him like a tiger in a pit."

"Bad luck, aye, Simons?" asked Garrett.

"Damned bad luck," replied Simons.

"Yes, particularly bad luck," said Garrett casually, "he had four hundred better horses back in his stables at Rokeby."

Chapter Twelve

> I have no spur
> To prick the sides of my intent, but only
> Vaulting ambition, which o'erleaps itself
> And falls on th' other.
>
> — *Macbeth*

The Carancahua community was deeply saddened by the list of casualties from the battle of Shiloh. Almost every family had either a brother, son, uncle or husband in the army, either in Virginia or in the West, and so everyone could sympathize with those who had suffered a loss. George Brackenridge had not joined Federal army, but neither had he joined the Confederates. This did not endear him to his neighbors. In the early months of the war, when the Confederates were winning battles in Virginia, the locals would, when encountering George, 'hurrah' him about being a Yankee. Then, after Shiloh, the same people would pass him without speaking, and he could hear them talking about him after they passed.

Old John Adams Brackenridge had died, without having achieved his quest of acquiring Rokeby Heights from Clark Owen. It would be up to his sons now to fulfill their father's dream. However, with Owen killed at Shiloh, an opportunity now presented itself to his son George Brackenridge. The firm of Brackenridge and Bates, who now included George, had formed an informal business relationship with Charles Stillman. Stillman was a well-known businessman in this area of Texas, who had exploited the current situation, and became wealthy as a result.

George Billups, the brother of the Sea Captain, too old to actively serve, was the enrolling agent in Jackson County for the Confederate Army, in charge of making sure all able-bodied men were serving in the army. As such, he paid a visit to George Brackenridge in the days following Shiloh.

"Why, sir, are you not in the army?" was Billups's blunt interrogatory.

" I am too busy with my business interests now. Please grant me an exemption."

"The word on the street is that you are in league with Stillman," said Billups.

" What if I am?"

"How do you expect to avoid the blockade of the North, and the

South's embargo?"

"My dear Billups, any man who can get cotton to Mexico, can send it to market, with little thought for either the Northern blockade or the Southern embargo. Charles Stillman has made the transfer of goods from one side of the Rio Grande to the other, into a fine art," said Brackenridge.

"Smuggling, you mean?" said Billups with a wry smile.

"Stillman is the foremost enterprising businessman operating establishments in both cities facing the river: Matamoros and Brownsville," said Brackenridge.

"The Confederate officer at Pass Cavallo (the entrance to Matagorda Bay) has observed the constant run of small craft taking out large exports of cotton and sugar and bringing back salt, coffee and other supplies," said Billups.

To this, Brackenridge merely smiled but said nothing.

"Nevertheless, some of your business practices are none too popular with people," said Billups.

"We are refusing Confederate paper in settlement of accounts, and in exchange for merchandise, insist on gold or cotton," said Brackenridge.

"I suppose you call that good business," said Billups.

"I cannot afford to allow my emotions to overrule my business sense."

Billups, thoroughly disgusted with Brackenridge, terminated the conversation with terse words: " I see … well good day, sir," said Billups.

It was not too long after this conversation, that George Brackenridge left Jackson County and headed east to the Federal capital, Washington City, where he was given a place in the Treasury Department.

Brackenridge returned to Texas about a year later, this time as a Federal agent with broad control over commerce in the areas of Texas occupied by Federal forces. He was authorized to issue permits for trade, to take possession of and manage abandoned plantations and other property, and to receive abandoned and captured cotton for forwarding to New Orleans. Brackenridge used his official position to help Charles Stillman acquire and ship his cotton.

" If the Federals can just establish a foothold here in Jackson County," thought George, "then I would have the run of the county, and with all the young men off to war, would be in fine position to make Rokeby my own!"

Chapter Thirteen

Cry 'Havoc!' and let slip the dogs of war.

— *Julius Caesar*

Richard Austin Howard, having attended the Military Academy at West Point, New York, several years earlier, had made several friendships that resulted in his being sought after and admitted into the Confederate army at the outbreak of hostilities. He was offered a position on Colonel Earl Van Dorn's staff.

He proceeded to pack his bags, which included borrowing some books from the little cottage at Rokeby. As he packed his belongings away, he expressed his thoughts to old Joe, Clark Owen's servant, who was helping him gather various equipment and firearms for the war.

"Ah envy you, Marse Richard, if ah was a lettle bit younga man, ah would tak up mah musket an folla you boys goin'ta whip the Yankees," said Joe with a big smile.

"You stay here and take care of Rokeby for Colonel Owen. I am afraid the future will bring some dire circumstances around here. The people will need all the help they can get," said Howard.

He mused silently as he packed a homemade uniform and warm clothing for the winters.

"Besides, Joe, what is there in my situation to envy? Cast off, having grown up without parents, my adoptive parents not having the means to properly care for me or educate me or train me to a skill. Dependent upon the generosity of others for everything. I failed to acquire a commission in the army, failed to graduate …," sputtered Howard, in a fit of self-pity.

"Whar you figure you'll go?" asked Joe.

"Colonel Van Dorn was kind enough to invite me to join his staff. I suspect we will be busy 'acquiring' all the Federal military property in Texas for the new provisional southern army. Perhaps the Northern States will let us leave the Union in peace, but … I doubt it."

"By acquiring you mean stealin' doncha?" asked Joe.

"Yes," laughed Howard, "alright … you have me there, yes stealing."

"God bless you, Marse Richard, an' keep you in His protection," said Joe with tears in his eyes.

"Thank you, Joe. I will miss you too, yes, all your tomfoolery. Now, could you hand me Caesar's Commentaries off the shelf there?"

or The Maid of Saragoza

Joe handed him the two leather bound books with gilt edging and red decoration on them, and Howard stuffed them into his haversack.

"Are de Yankees afraid uv Col'nel Van Dorn?" said Joe.

"Well, they should be if they are not. I expect he has some surprises up his sleeve. The Yankees better be on guard and sleep with one eye open, or old Van Dorn will land a lightning strike!" said Howard.

Joe helped Howard saddle his horse and fasten all his baggage.

"Well, that should be all that I can carry. Joe, I will try and write to Miss Laura and I will remind her of what needs to be done throughout the year. Make sure all the animals keep fed and mind Miss Laura and the other ladies."

With that, Howard rode away to meet up with Van Dorn's command.

True to Howard's prediction, he was present when Van Dorn struck like a lightning bolt, and surprised the Federals in Texas, by capturing the Star of the West, the celebrated steamship that had drawn the actual first shots of the war, from the cadets in South Carolina.

Howard then left his staff position with Van Dorn and had gone to Virginia as a volunteer aide to General Bee. He was greeted upon his arrival by many of his friends who had gone to school with him at the Military Academy. Howard was carrying dispatches at the battle of First Manassas, in July of 1861, when he was desperately wounded, it was feared mortally, when he was hit by shrapnel from a cannon shot. He was nursed back to health after many months of care and rest. At length, the army transferred him, with the rank of Captain Commissary and Subsistence, to Texas and the Trans-Mississippi Department of the Confederate States Provisional Army. It was at this point that Howard commenced the career at which he was so justly celebrated, namely, the procuring and transporting of beef cattle from Texas, across the Mississippi, to General Lee's army in Virginia.

Chapter Fourteen

I desire to call your attention to these facts: — That I have been a soldier for nearly a quarter of a century; that my career has been an eventful one; that I have accumulated nothing of the world's wealth, having devoted my whole life and energies to the service of my country; and that, therefore, my reputation is all that belongs to me, without which life to me were as valueless as the crisp and faded leaf of autumn. ...

— Excerpt from General Van Dorn's Statement at the Inquiry following Corinth.

Colonel John Creed Moore was promoted to Brigadier General, following Shiloh, and William P. Rogers was now Colonel of the Second Texas. The energetic and phlegmatic Earl Van Dorn was placed in command of the Confederate "Army of West Tennessee." General Dabney Maury's division was a part of this Army and was made up of the brigades of General Phifer, Cabell, and Moore. Moore's brigade was comprised of the 42nd Alabama, 15th Arkansas, 35th Mississippi, 23rd Arkansas, Bledsoe's battery, and the Second Texas.

General Van Dorn is much maligned, and his name has been traduced by both professional and amateur historians, repeating second and third-hand information passed down through time of his dalliances with the attractive wife of Doctor Peters. His death by Doctor Peters has been cited as proof of Van Dorn's guilty relations with the said woman. His murder in Tennessee went unpunished and even uninvestigated by the local officials. It is true that some Generals down through time seem to reap good fortune, sometimes despite their actual shortcomings and mistakes, while others who have many virtues, seem to be maligned every step of the way. Van Dorn was certainly in the maligned class.

However, let us examine what his contemporaries thought of Van Dorn, specifically, what General Dabney Maury, a well-respected fellow Confederate General, known for his sagacity and truthfulness, thought of him. General Maury called Van Dorn, long after Van Dorn's death, and at a time when there would be no motive to misrepresent the facts, "the greatest man ever produced by the State of Mississippi."

A native of Port Gibson, Mississippi, Van Dorn was in the old Second (U. S.) Cavalry regiment, during the 1850's. A graduate of the U.S. Military Academy, he was dashing, gallant, wrote poetry, painted beautiful pictures, and was an aggressive fighter and Confederate devotee in the

J.E.B. Stuart mold. He was a rather diminutive man in stature, although he made a fine figure on a horse. His hair was blonde and curly and worn in the typical long fashion of the times. He was a daring and fearless cavalry officer, but was unlucky as a commander, as the events of Elkhorn Tavern and Corinth would prove. Van Dorn's plan for seizing Corinth was a sound one, and he came very close to capturing the place.

The reader must remember that the Yankees occupied Corinth, not the other way around. Following the battle of Shiloh, Beauregard chose to abandon Corinth, and retreat southward, rather than stand a siege. Thus, the old Confederate line of fortifications were now occupied by Federal soldiers.

Van Dorn's plan for capturing Corinth was to march from Ripley to Pocahontas, feigning an attack on the Federal garrison at Bolivar. Then, the Confederates would rapidly veer eastward twenty miles to hopefully surprise and capture Corinth, before it could be reinforced. Hurlbut had 8000 troops at Bolivar, and Rosecrans had 15,000 at Corinth. The old Confederate line of fortifications, two-and one-half miles from Corinth, ran in an arc which extended from the northwest to the east. Rosecrans had built another, inner, system of breastworks and siege gun emplacements on the western periphery. Two key gun emplacements, called Battery Robinett and Battery Williams, were part of the inner line of works, on the northwest side of Corinth, less than a mile outside the town. Van Dorn's plan was reliant on celerity, however, Rosecrans learned of the approach of the Confederates, and concentrated 25,000 troops at Corinth, to await the arrival of the Rebel host.

Many historians censure Van Dorn, for attacking fixed fortifications, but it must be remembered that he was the last Confederate commander to launch an offensive campaign in Mississippi. Van Dorn's plan was nothing if not bold: once he had destroyed the Federal army in the West, at Corinth, he was going north to capture St. Louis, and then invade Illinois!

It was General Van Dorn who was in command and successfully defeated the Federal navy at Vicksburg, in June of 1862. It was also General Van Dorn who was responsible for pushing forward the plans to unleash the ironclad CSS *Arkansas* against the Federal fleet near Vicksburg.

However, earlier in the year, a bold maneuver by Van Dorn at Elk Horn Tavern, (attempting to have two separate bodies of the army to rejoin together and crush the enemy), unfortunately failed, and the Confederacy's bid to oust the Federals from Arkansas came to naught.

Van Dorn suffered much ignominy as a result of base rumor as to his private life. Although he had a buoyant spirit, by the time of the Corinth campaign, he was disenchanted. About this time, he called for Colonel Thomas Waul, of the Waul Texas Legion, during one of these down periods. Upon arrival at his headquarters, General Van Dorn bid Waul to have a seat.

"Colonel Waul," said Van Dorn, "a few kind-hearted and patriotic little schoolgirls of my native town, Port Gibson, Mississippi, have sent me a hundred pairs of fine woolen socks, knit by their own hands, to be distributed to the Texas soldiers of my command," as he motioned towards a large crate of socks sitting on the floor.

"Please accept them for your Legion, and give them to those most in need," said Van Dorn.

Colonel Waul looked at the letter which had accompanied the socks.

"You will observe that these little angels identify me with Texas. … They are right! I am a Texan, a Mississippian no longer, except in my love for the pure-hearted children of her soil who have not yet learned to make the name and fame of one of her sons the butt of malignant archery," said Van Dorn.

Then he smiled and added: "Bless them, they belong to no State, neither are they cosmopolitan, they are of heaven."

"Thank you, General," replied Colonel Waul, "We soldiers do not take notice of base falsehood and the malicious and unjustified harming of a person's good reputation. There are always going to be some people who love to tear down other persons who, to their small minds, have ascended to heights more properly occupied by them. You can always count on the Texas Legion, General. I will ensure that the socks are dispersed to my soldiers."

Prior to the attack on Corinth, the Federals had attempted to trap General Sterling Price's army at Iuka. However, this time it was the Yankees who failed to smash the Confederates in a pincer movement. The Second Texas had performed a conspicuous part, in the laying of an ambush of a part of the Federal army that was trailing the Confederates, after the battle.

Now, General Sterling Price would join his army with Van Dorn's army, and together they would go on the offensive, to be under the overall command of Van Dorn. The two armies together totaled about 22,000 soldiers.

The Confederates attacked on the first day of the battle of Corinth, October 3rd, and carried the "outer," or "old Confederate" line, of defensive works. The Rebel army slept on their arms that night, on the outskirts of the town of Corinth. The element of surprise, which General Van Dorn had hoped to take advantage of, would not be available due to several delays encountered by the Confederates on their march.

General Van Dorn held a meeting with division commanders the night before the planned resumption of attack on the 4th of October. Van Dorn was in outwardly fine spirits and exuded a feeling of confidence. He addressed his good friend General Dabney Maury: "Maury, old boy, your intrepid division has been assigned to capture the key position of Battery Robinett and pierce the center of the Federal line. Look at this map…," said General Van Dorn, as he proceeded to lay before the assembled officers a map showing the defensive works at Corinth and explained how he came to possess it.

"This map was found on the battle-field of Iuka. It details the shape, size and location of the inner line of fortifications at Corinth. Even naming the batteries. Your objective will be Battery Robinett, and I know you and Colonel Rogers, and your Texas, Arkansas and Mississippi regiments are second to none in courage and devotion to the country. I have no doubt of your carrying the place," said General Van Dorn.

"There is a clear field of fire, under which we will be subject to their artillery shells for quite some time," observed Colonel Rogers.

"Yes, although I know that where Rogers leads, his Texans will follow," added Van Dorn.

"Is the map an elaborate ruse?" questioned Colonel Rogers.

"No, by good fortune, you see the name of the engineer that prepared it, he happens to be from the same hometown as one of my men, and my man knows his signature," replied General Van Dorn.

Then General Van Dorn proceeded to give instructions to the other officers assembled, for the next morning attack on the "inner," and more formidable, and more recently constructed Federal works. The Second Texas, in Maury's division, was to attack Stanley's Federal division in the center. General Hebert's division was assigned the task of outflanking Davies on the Federal right. General Lovell's division was to attack McKean on the Federal left.

General Van Dorn asked General Dabney Maury to stay behind after he had dismissed the others.

"Maury, old boy, I know I can always count on your friendship. The reason I have asked you to stay behind is, frankly, I have had a premonition that I may not survive the attack tomorrow."

"General, you always have my friendship and respect, but you know how baseless those premonitions of death can be. …"

"Yes, but we also know of instances where they have been true, " replied Van Dorn.

"Nevertheless, I would counsel you, General, not to credit them."

"Maury, you have never let me down or tried to undermine my efforts, I cannot say the same for my other Generals."

"I am sure they are loyal to you," said Maury.

"No! I am sorry to say, some of them are not! and that is why I have asked you to stay behind, so that I may explain my reasons for attacking a fortified line tomorrow," said Van Dorn.

Then he paused, and the features of his face changed from his usual aplomb, and become strained, and his eyebrows become knit in a slight frown of anxiety.

"Maury, if I do not survive the attack tomorrow, you must know. … Maury our fledgling nation has a limited amount of time in which to win its Independence. Those of my Generals who counsel: 'the enemy will cut us to shreds, we must withdraw and attack at some other opportunity…' (Van Dorn pounded his fist into his other hand for emphasis) …"WHEN? What better opportunity? Wait? Wait for what? Until we have less men than we do now? We hardly have enough to perform these minor offensive operations. Wait? Wait for Richmond to send us more men? It will not happen. (Mocking Richmond:) 'You must do with what you have,' A year, six months from now, we will have less men, and we barely have enough to clothe and feed them now. What will we have six months from now?"

Maury was not expecting such admissions from General Van Dorn, who normally affected a demeanor of confidence and positiveness. He said nothing.

"Maury, when I am in my grave, you must tell our countrymen that this was my reason. …"

"Of course, General, of course," said Maury. "Now let's get some rest."

Early the next morning, the morning of the attack on the inner fortifications, Colonel William P. Rogers looked at the daunting Yankee defenses, through a field glass, as the Confederates formed up in the woods facing the town.

"There is a clear field of fire about 400 yards wide. I see a most obstructive abatis of tree branches, sharpened into points, and interlaced with wires," said Colonel Rogers to his staff officers.

"Behind the abatis, to the east, is Battery Robinett, with six-foot-high walls. The fort has at least three siege guns. Battery Williams, south of Robinett, is close enough to Robinett to enable either fort to support an attack on the other," the Colonel further said.

The sun continued to rise above the horizon in the East, and the soldiers of the Second Texas formed for the assault that they all knew was inevitable, and the clash of arms, which they had experienced many times before, and were feeling the usual sensation of a knot in the pit in their stomachs, that time had not erased. The outlines of Battery Robinett were clear in the distance, as were the blue lines of Federals that stretched on either side of the works in a long line. Behind this spectacle could be seen the spires of the churches and the houses of Corinth.

The jolly rotund Frankie Burwell was studying the outlines of Battery Robinett through a glass that one of the officers had produced. After he had finished looking through the glass, he handed it back to the officer. He turned to William Stayton and asked:

"Say, Will, that battery has a fearsome look to it, do you know of a good way to charge a battery?"

"Fool!" laughed Stayton, "there ain't no good way to charge a battery!"

The Second Texas stood in line at attention, facing the town. The regiment was still clothed in the undyed cotton jeans jackets with a nine-button front and stand-up collar, which appeared to be in a quite filthy and ragged condition. Their trousers appeared to be of undyed cotton or wool jeans showing heavy campaigning. On their heads most of the men still wore the wide-brimmed slouch hats they had left Texas with.

Colonel Rogers heard one of the men, looking at the long lines of blue uniforms flanking Battery Robinett, say: "I wish to G_d we had but one fifth of those men that lay abed in Texas today!"

Colonel Rogers, hearing this, shouted out in a loud voice, as he rode his horse along the line of soldiers preparing to assault:

"What do I hear? No! Not one man more! I would not wish a man more here than I have. No, my men! If we are to die here today, we are enough to do our country loss, and if to live, the fewer men, the greater the share of honor! He that has no stomach for this fight, let him depart! We would not die in that man's company that fears to die with us!"

Then, he said: "This is the Fourth of October … he that outlives this day will one day swell up with pride when this day is named and will yearly feast his family and neighbors and say, 'tomorrow is the Fourth of October,' then he will show his scars, and say, 'these wounds I had at the Battle of Corinth', and he shall recount what feats of bravery he did that day. Then shall our names be remembered in story and in song. The story of this battle shall the father teach his son, and the Fourth of October shall never go by, but our names shall be remembered on it! … And gentlemen in Texas now a-bed shall think themselves accursed they were not here; and hold their manhood cheap when our women say with pride: my father, brother, fought with Rogers and the Second Texas, at the great battle of CORINTH!"

With this, the men let out a great cheer, as Colonel Rogers prepared to give the command to charge.

With the coming of the dawn, the Federal Forts Williams, Robinett, and College Hill had all opened a terrific cannonade of shot and shell, directed toward the Confederate columns. The Texans had laid down in a skirt of woods about 400 yards away from Robinett. The signal gun for the Confederates was fired at 10:00 o'clock a.m. The Confederate left flank, General Hebert's division, did not lead the attack despite General Van Dorn's specific order. It was later discovered that General Hebert reported himself "sick," but only after one crucial hour had already passed. The responsibility devolved upon General Green, who unfortunately had never been included in the specific plan of attack by General Hebert, and consequently, this occasioned a further delay.

Thus, Moore's brigade, of which the Second Texas was a part, attacked without the assistance of Hebert's division, and thus the Confederate attack was materially impaired.

Captain George Foster, of company "D" of the 42nd Alabama, striding toward Battery Robinett, and attempting to motivate his men, shouted: "They (referring to the Texans) shan't beat us to those breastworks, **FORWARD ALABAMIANS!**"

The Texans raised the rebel yell and were now about fifty yards away from the clear ground directly in front of Battery Robinett. The abatis was terrible and obstructive, and the men climbed over and around the fallen trees and limbs. Battery Robinett now changed shells for grape and canister. Minies were now flying about the heads of the attackers. The colors of the 42nd Alabama fell, and then were snatched up, and carried on.

Three times the Texans charged, and three times they were driven back, before they finally broke through to Robinett. Colonel Rogers himself carried the colors of the Second Texas, mounted on a black horse, up to the Fort. Now the Confederates were just feet away from the Fort, the ranks significantly thinned. The gunners inside the Fort now changed to whole bags of buckshot. Hand grenades came flying over the walls of the Fort.

"Pick them up, boys, and pitch them back into the Fort," said one of the Rebel officers. "Over the walls, and drive them out," he shouted. There commenced a horrible hand-to-hand combat in which the men were

or The Maid of Saragoza

seen to be using their bayonets to run through the enemy combatants, like farmers use their pitchforks to put up hay.

The Yankees were now running back toward the town. The Confederates entered the Fort and saw various Federals who had been slain or were dying, including the brave Lieutenant Robinett, shot in the head.

The Confederates who had managed to reach Robinett, among them Colonel Rogers and Captain Foster, stood beside the Fort, when suddenly approached a wave of fifteen hundred Federal muskets. Colonel Rogers, realizing the inevitable, tied a white cloth to his rammer, and waved it, vainly endeavoring to surrender. It was at that moment that some Confederate fired his gun into the blue line, and in the return fire, the little group of rebels standing there were dropped in a heap. Colonel Rogers was among the slain, having been pierced by multiple balls.

Meanwhile, Phifer's brigade of Maury's Division, had captured Battery Powell, and even got some men in the town itself. Rosecrans was on the verge of destroying the ammunition stores in the town and retreating, when suddenly fortunes changed, and it became evident that the Confederates had failed in their attempt to capture Corinth.

Hebert's division finally moved forward under the bewildered General Green, but the lack of coordination with Maury's attack, doomed the Confederates. Meanwhile, General Lovell, commanding a division, could not be found, and General Bowen, commanding one of his brigades, could only repeatedly send back messages to Lovell to see if he were to advance. No such order came until it was clear that Maury and Green had been repulsed, and then it was rescinded.

Thus, Maury's division alone was left to carry the effort to capture the town. Of the approximately four thousand troops Maury took into the battle, over two thousand were killed, wounded or captured — and half of these belonged to Moore's brigade. In the Second Texas, there were ten killed, thirty-four wounded, and one hundred twenty-two missing.

It was evident that Lovell and Hebert had refused to do their duty, apparently not willing to make a frontal assault on fixed fortifications. However, the Confederates having come so close to capturing the town, makes one sanguine of the chances, had Hebert and Lovell committed their troops as they had been ordered. Hebert failed to file a report of the battle. Lovell, who earlier in the war had been blamed for surrendering New Orleans without a fight, was, after Corinth, quietly assigned to a meaningless post. Van Dorn never addressed these two instances of failure to obey orders in his official report, presumably because it would destroy fighting spirit to acknowledge that a Confederate general refused to carry out a direct order.

General Bowen later preferred charges against Van Dorn, for alleged incompetence and mistreatment of his men, although these charges were completely baseless. Van Dorn was absolved of all charges at the inquiry. Nevertheless, the accusations were left to resonate with the people, and Van Dorn was relegated to commanding cavalry raids, for which he proved to have a decided talent, for the balance of his service to the Confederacy.

Colonel Rogers was buried by the Yankees, with military honors, a few paces from where he fell, at the side of Battery Robinett. His grave was marked, at General Rosecrans' order, so that his family could later claim his body. Yet his family refrained to move his body, deeming this a worthy location for his final resting place.

General Van Dorn paid high tribute to Colonel Rogers in his official report:

... I cannot refrain, however, from mentioning here the conspicuous gallantry of a noble Texan, whose deeds at Corinth are the constant theme of both friends and foes. As long as courage, manliness, fortitude, patriotism, and honor exist the name of Rogers will be revered and honored among men. He fell in the front of battle, and died beneath the colors of his regiment, in the very center of the enemy's stronghold. He sleeps, and glory is his sentinel.

Company K lost Sergeant J. M. B. Haynie, and six privates, who were killed when some of the 42nd Alabama mistakenly fired into Company K. J. A. Bolling, whose family lived at the confluence of the two Carancahuas, was killed at Corinth.

Chapter Fifteen

Down the Matagorda Bay, flow the waters smooth and shallow,
Gaining fleetness on the way, hurrying down to Pass Cavallo,
In and outward, night and day, pushing through the Pass Cavallo —
Lost in foaming ocean spray, round the gate of Pass Cavallo.
— *Soldiers Song of Pass Cavallo*

When Galveston harbor fell to Federal naval forces on October 4, 1862, the denizens of Jackson County knew it was only a matter of time before they would probe into the Matagorda Bay. On October 25th, Federal gunboats appeared off Pass Cavallo. The Confederates attempted unsuccessfully to turn the ships back from Fort Esperanza (a fort placed by the Confederates at the Pass Cavallo). The distant booming of the fort's cannons was heard by the residents of the important port of Indianola.

Indianola fell, after a brief fight, and the Federals moved toward Port Lavaca. The enemy demanded surrender, which was refused. Women and children were allowed to evacuate the town. After much damage to Port Lavaca from the Yankee bombardment, the Federal naval ships moved on toward the Lavaca and Navidad rivers.

The heavy firing at Port Lavaca was now heard by the citizens of Jackson County, and they realized that the Yankees had indeed, "come." The local militia were called out, but these militiamen consisted of exempt men (unable for some physical reason to serve) and those too old for active campaigning.

Mrs. Lizzie Simons, wife of Maurice K. Simons, the Major and Commissary, wrote in her diary for October 28, 1862: "Great excitement about the Yanks. Milam's (her brother's) company gone to Carancahua Bay scouting. Militia ordered out (to) go to Lavaca … Our theme all day & all evening as we sit round the table at work is the Yankees."

The ranches and plantations in Jackson County were suffering from the Federal blockade on the Gulf. However, the sleek little "blockade runners" occasionally were able to slip past the Federal gunships, outbound with cotton and hides, and inbound with arms and ammunition, coffee, and tools.

George Brackenridge, now a representative of the Federal authority, could again show his face in Jackson County, as the Northerners began to assemble an occupation force. His business interests affiliated with

Charles Stillman, were reaping handsome war profits, as well. After Clark Owen's death at Shiloh, his beautiful plantation home, Rokeby, had been operated by his widow, Mrs. Laura Owen, a fine southern lady, but no match for the unscrupulous and scheming Brackenridge. Shortages and the devaluation of money were making life at Rokeby difficult. With there being no dependable men around to supervise the day-to-day operations, the farming and business interests at Rokeby were gradually collapsing into chaos. Brackenridge had on behalf of the creditors of Mrs. Owen, foreclosed on the mortgages he and other creditors held against Rokeby. This included falsified reports he had concocted about the farming and ranching operations at Rokeby. Eventually, he had arranged for him to take title to the entire two-thousand acres, including the manor house and gardens on Rokeby Heights.

The Federals, as a prelude to invasion, had marched a reconnaissance-in-force, unopposed, up the Lavaca and Navidad rivers, not far from Rokeby. George Brackenridge was present with the Federal officer commanding the force, a Colonel Archibald Hagenbach, serving him as a guide and advisor. Upon their arrival, the first thing Colonel Hagenbach asked was where he could locate the rebel, R. A. Howard?

"I do not know where he is, but I suggest you interview one of the loyal servants on the plantations," answered Brackenridge.

"Whose plantation is this?" Hagenbach asked.

"This is Rokeby, home of the late Captain Clark Owen, who was killed at Shiloh," replied Brackenridge.

"However," he added, "I have acquired title to the entire two thousand acres."

Brackenridge assured Hagenbach that he and his troops were welcome to camp on the grounds of Rokeby. A half-hour passed, and Colonel Hagenbach, having returned to Rokeby, told Brackenridge:

"The rebel Howard cannot be found in the vicinity. In time we will capture him. For now, we will be marching back to the gunboats. We will, however, be returning to Jackson County, in several months, as part of the van of the army invading Texas."

The reason for singling out Richard Austin Howard, was never divulged by Colonel Hagenbach.

"Now, bring in the contraband!" ordered Colonel Hagenbach.

Into the tent was led one of the Negroes from Rokeby.

"Now, we are here to liberate you, and as part of that process, we wish to learn what information you might have to help us when we invade this God-forsaken place," said Colonel Hagenbach.

"Specifically, do you know where I might find Major R. A. Howard, the notorious rebel?"

The Negro sat silent and sullen.

"Confound it, do you not understand who I represent?"

"Yes, marse, you from de Linkum gun-boats in de ha'ba," said the negro.

"Yes, and we are here to liberate your dirty black hide. Now, will you help us?" asked Hagenbach.

Again, the Negro sat silent, and stared at the floor.

One of the young staff officers spoke at this time: "He ran from us. We had to capture him after a long chase. He refused to accompany us!" he said exasperatedly.

"Evidently he misunderstood who we are," reasoned Hagenbach.

"Now, sir, we are bringing our armies here in several months. You know these people around here, this part of Texas. Tell us, will they fight?"

The negro paused, had a long, thoughtful look on his face, and finally responded with a grin: "Oh yes, marse, dey will fight you like de debel."

At this expression, Hagenbach was observed to turn sullen, was at a loss for words, and his face reddened. There was a long silence, and the Federal Colonel Hagenbach shouted, in an irritated voice: "Begone with this … man!"

After Brackenridge left, Colonel Hagenbach gave orders to break camp and prepare to march.

Meanwhile, at the same time this scene was transpiring, a strange occurrence was taking place on the nearby plantation of Victor LaBauve. The servant and Seer, Flora, in the middle of performing some domestic tasks, suddenly stopped what she was doing, and appeared to be in a trance. Somehow, Flora's visionary gift made her aware of the presence of the Yankee reconnaissance-in-force.

The other negroes that were with her saw her make some strange hand gestures and consult an old tome. Then she was heard to say: "The Yankees are marching back to their boats tonight in the dark. By the mysteries of Hecate and the Night, confusion to their columns! By the operation of the orbs, from whom we do exist, bring on their ruin! Hecate, to whom crossroads are sacred, place a crossroads in their path! Bird of the Night, harbinger of ill omen, announce thine presence!"

Several miles away, the Yankee column followed closely the map they had been provided by Brackenridge, as the sun began to set below the horizon. While still light, an owl landed on a tree limb overhanging the road, on which the Yankees marched. The bird hooted and shrieked. Some of the soldiers blurted out: "See the bird of the Night, hooting in the daytime, 'tis a bad omen!"

"Quiet in the ranks!" shouted the sergeant.

"Lieutenant," said Colonel Hagenbach, to the staff officers riding beside him, "I do not recall this crossroads on our march up here, and it is not on the infernal map! D__n this benighted country! Can they not even draw a simple map of their roads?" he asked rhetorically.

Night fell, and along the now dark road the column was marching, there suddenly rang out gunshots from the back of the ranks! Then there were screams of men in intense pain. A mad stampede then took place, as the soldiers ran, most disgracefully, for the safety of the gunboats.

That they had been attacked, there was no doubt. Depending upon who was asked, there were varying opinions as to the identity of the attackers, or even the number of them. Some said it was an animal, perhaps a wolf; some said they were Southern partisans; and some said it was a human-like creature of a short but stout stature, with animal-like strength. One thing that was certain, whoever the attacker was, he had escaped, and several of the Federal soldiers had been killed in the ambush.

Chapter Sixteen

In Nature's poem flowers have each their word
The rose of love and beauty sings alone,
The violet's soul exhales in tenderest tone,
The lily's one pure simple note heard.
The cold Camellia only, stiff and white,
Rose without perfume, lily without grace,
When chilling winter shows his icy face,
Blooms for a world that vainly seeks delight.

— *The Camellia*

Major R. A. Howard was in fact in Jackson County, despite the inability of the Yankee Colonel to locate him. He was again in the process of organizing another cattle drive across the Mississippi, for the army in Virginia. He kept a low profile after learning of the presence of the Federals, and their demand for information concerning his whereabouts. He was disappointed that the Federal intelligence service had uncovered what he had hoped were veiled operations on behalf of the Confederacy.

Once he had determined the Yankees had left and had embarked on their boats on the Navidad River, he hurried to the building in Texana he used as an office. Waiting in the office were two of his staff officers, who had escorted one of the local doctors of the community, Dr. James Woolfork, to meet with Major Howard.

"Would you please come here and sit down," Major Howard told the doctor.

"My name is Major R. A. Howard, of the Confederate States Army. My orders come from General Kirby Smith. He commands in this jurisdiction. You are in the Reserve Corps, are you not?" he asked.

"Yes, a year ago I served with the army at Shiloh, as a medical officer."

"Yes, I have your file… Doctor James Woolfork, a graduate of the medical school at Louisville, served at Shiloh with the Second Texas, administering medical aid to our wounded. Received a commendation for your actions at Shiloh. I say, good show. Very well."

Howard lit his fine meerschaum pipe filled with the good Turkish tobacco and leaned back his chair.

"I presume my staff has enlightened you as to the reason you are here?" asked Howard.

"I guessed, knowing you to be a Commissary-Subsistence officer, you wish for me to accompany your men and render medical services?" asked Woolfork.

One of Howard's staff officers interrupted: "Actually we had not yet had the opportunity to explain to the Doctor what. …"

Howard gave an irritated look at the staff officer, then turned back to Woolfork and said:

"Doctor Woolfork, have you ever heard of the Order of the Red Camellia?"

" No," said the Doctor.

"The Order of the Red Camellia is a secret organization that exists in the Southern army. It originally was founded by some staff officers of General Van Dorn's who took it upon themselves to avenge his murder. His murder was never investigated by either the civil or the military authorities, and no one was ever put on trial or even charged. And so, the Order of the Red Camellia was born, and it served its purpose. Having completed that original purpose, it became an organization that encouraged and attempted to influence the course of the war in the Southern army. The members are known to each other by the wearing of a red camellia on the lapel of the jacket..."

"What does all this have to do with me?" interrupted Woolfork.

"As I was saying, this secret organization makes suggestions and attempts to influence the war. We are interested in unorthodox, but effective, methods and modes of fighting the war. Our objective is to win the war, however and whatever is necessary."

"Where does General Lee stand with this organization?" asked Woolfork.

"He knows of it, does not oppose it, but felt his position was a conflicting one, so he is not a member."

"Who else is a member?" asked Woolfork.

"Doctor Woolfork, I will be blunt. We are needing your assistance in a program of the utmost importance to the country. It is a matter cloaked in secrecy, for reasons that, I trust, will appear obvious," said Howard in a serious manner, "Do you have experience with the transmission of diseases from cattle?"

"I have some experience in treating bovine diseases, as a result of being a stock raiser in Jackson County, of course, but. …"

Howard then interrupted the Doctor: "This program has been assigned to me by the very highest level of the government. Do you understand? The very highest."

"I am afraid I do not understand your meaning," said Woolfork.

"We do not want you to cure or treat disease in cattle. We are developing a program to infect animals, cattle, with disease, but keep them on the hoof and moving, until the cattle can be driven into the enemies' camp. …"

"Until" interrupted Woolfork, "they can be captured by the enemy and thereby consumed by the Federal troops, and the disease spread?"

"Yes," responded Howard.

"Have you any army doctors that believed such a thing was possible? I would think that a tall order," said Woolfork, as Howard handed him several heavy tomes of a medical and scientific nature, including works on Bovine Diseases, and Transmission and Treatment of Various Animal Diseases.

Woolfork was silent for a period of time, while he examined the medical books.

"Major," said Woolfork finally, "I am not a military man, having only had the experience of treating our men at the Battle of Shiloh. But even I know that after the war ends, whichever side prevails, the winning side will conduct hearings on the conduct of the war, and into…deviations from the… accepted rules of civilized warfare."

"Do you think it is a deviation?" said Howard, smiling slightly.

The doctor remained silent.

"The ancient world provides us precedent, does it not, Doctor?" asked Howard: "did not, during the Trojan War, the combatants tip their spears and arrows with poison? Did not the Hittites drive victims of plague into enemy hands?" Did not Hannibal of Carthage fill pots of venomous snakes and have them thrown onto the decks of ships?"

"What you are asking of me I fear exceeds my poor understanding of the subject," stated Woolfork.

Howard ignored the doctor's protestations and continued: "I have the resources of the government at my disposal in this operation. I am assembling other doctors from other parts of the Confederacy. There are no official records being kept, as this operation is totally secret; you will destroy all evidence as you go along and especially at the conclusion of the project."

" And if I decline?"

" I would think that, now that you know about the Order of the Red Camellia, about this project, that we would hope that you would commit to this program so as to avoid any unwarranted disclosure."

" Very well, Major, I accept your offer, am I to stay here or be posted

or The Maid of Saragoza

somewhere else?"

"A messenger will contact you, Doctor, with that information shortly."

And thus, the very strange meeting between Richard Austin Howard and Doctor Woolfork concluded.

Chapter Seventeen

*The evacuation of Vicksburg! It would mean the
loss of valuable stores of munitions of war collected
for its defense, the fall of Port Hudson, the surrender
of the Mississippi River, and the severance of the Confederacy!*
— General Pemberton's Speech To His Men.

The reader is no doubt aware of the many schemes attempted by General Grant to capture the "Gibraltar of the South," the "City of the Hills," ... Vicksburg, in the latter part of 1862 and the early months of 1863.

Lieutenant-General John C. Pemberton, who replaced General Van Dorn, was assigned to defend Vicksburg, yet his responsibilities were far more complex than merely that task.

General Joseph E. Johnston was Pemberton's immediate superior and was charged with the Confederate war effort in the west, encompassing a large geographic area, in both Tennessee and Mississippi. Johnston's heart was simply not in his work, and his real desire was to be commanding the army in his native Virginia. General Lee, however, had replaced Johnston after Johnston was severely wounded at Seven Pines, and Lee's success insured that Johnston would not be returning to his former command of what was now called the Army of Northern Virginia. Johnston, whose headquarters was established at Chattanooga, essentially occupied himself with the efforts in Tennessee, and left Pemberton alone to face Grant in Mississippi. However, in early May 1863, Johnston was peremptorily ordered (by President Davis) to go to Mississippi in person and lend his supposed expertise to the matters quickly unfolding in Mississippi. Johnston preferred to abandon Vicksburg if necessary, rather than stand a siege, and to march the Vicksburg army out of their fortifications and maneuver, to lure the Yankees to fight on good defensive ground, and perhaps before the Yankees could concentrate all their component parts.

General Joe Johnston's approach to war was to sacrifice geographical "fixed locations" if it allowed his army to maneuver to perhaps attack the Federals on advantageous ground. This military philosophy might sound good in theory. The problem was that General Johnston never seemed to find that "good ground," and always seemed to be merely avoiding a battle.

Pemberton had been ordered by the President to hold Vicksburg at any cost, and besides which, Pemberton considered the strategic location of Vicksburg to be the most important point in the Confederacy. If Vicksburg held out, the Confederacy could thwart the navigation of the Mississippi River by the Federals. Thus, the dilemma Pemberton faced was conflicting orders between his superior, Johnston, and President Davis.

Vicksburg was located on a hairpin turn of the Mississippi and on high, sloping bluffs. The geography of the location made it supremely defensible from attack on the land, (or eastern), side, and General Pemberton had his chief engineer, Major Lockett, construct a line of entrenchments on the crests of a line of hills, extending in a semi-circle completely around the city, and about a mile in its rear. The uneven, hilly topography made it amenable to the construction of truly formidable redans, redoubts, and lunettes at locations where the key roads (such as the Jackson road or the Graveyard road) entered the Confederate line of entrenchments. Each fortification was then connected to each other by a line of rifle pits.

The Federal navy had complete mastery of the Mississippi at that time and was able to run the gauntlet of the Vicksburg river batteries, by running late at night, in the dark, and by going downstream (with the current) only. The Yankees lashed large barges filled with coal and forage to the actual transports, and placed cotton bales on them, to further protect them from the fire of the river batteries. The transport barges were needed by Grant to carry the large body of troops that would capture Vicksburg, from the Louisiana side to the Mississippi side.

Those various schemes of Grant had, prior to the night of April 16-17, 1863, been complete failures. On that night, however, seven gunboats, three transports, and one ram, ran the Vicksburg batteries.

Prior to the night of April 16-17, Grant had first attempted a direct advance south down the railroad from Memphis via Holly Springs, toward Grenada. However, the separate raids of Van Dorn and Forrest, upon Grant's communications, both in December of 1862, effectively caused Grant to retreat.

Next came Sherman's unsuccessful attack on Chickasaw Bayou, north of Vicksburg, in December of 1862. Sherman was repulsed with one brigade of the Vicksburg garrison.

After that Grant tried to send his boats down through Lake Providence, which failed because of natural impediments.

In March and April of 1863, Grant's gunboats were sent down some of the smaller rivers that joined up with Mississippi, but were repulsed at Fort Pemberton, a cotton-bale fort built with slave labor, at the junction of the Tallahatchie and Yalobusha rivers, located about ninety-five miles north of Vicksburg. The Second Texas had comprised part of the 1,500 Confederates sent there by General Pemberton.

Lastly, General Sherman and Admiral Porter unsuccessfully tried to reach the Sunflower and Yazoo Rivers, above Snyder's Bluff.

Thus, on the night of April 16-17, 1863, a large part of the upper fleet ran the Vicksburg batteries. This was once thought to be a suicidal gesture, considering the formidable nature of the Vicksburg batteries. Ironclad gunboats had frequently passed the Vicksburg batteries during the operations of the preceding ten months, but up to that time, no attempt to pass ordinary river steamboats, (without the protection of iron plating), had been thought possible. Now Grant had accomplished this feat and had the transports with which to ferry his troops across the river, south of Vicksburg.

The vigilant river defense system at Vicksburg consisted of some brave Confederates who volunteered to cross the river at night, in order to light fire to the piles of brush already soaked in flammable liquids, and thus to provide enough light to allow the gunners in the river batteries to see their targets. In doing so, these volunteers went beyond the ordinary call of valor: they were subject to being hit by their friends, the Confederate gunners, firing at the gunboats and transports. Yet they did their job calmly and effectively.

All seven gunboats, two transports, and the ram escaped the batteries at Vicksburg and at Warrenton. The *Henry Clay*, a transport, was sunk and two other boats were partially disabled, and several barges were sunk. However, ten total boats succeeded in getting past. "Once below Vicksburg," said Admiral Porter to General Grant, "the gun-boats cannot be sent back past Vicksburg." Even the powerful and protected gunboats, impeded by the current, would make them subject to Confederate battery fire for too long a period that even they could not survive.

Towards the end of April, Sherman made an attack at Snyder's Bluff, on the Yazoo River, and the Second Texas had been sent there, along with other veteran regiments, such as the Third Louisiana, to check any attempted attack on Vicksburg from the north. This movement by Sherman's force was merely a feint to create a diversion from the real crossing of Federals at Bruinsburg, south of Vicksburg, but the Confederates did not know this at the time.

General Pemberton was hampered by a lack of cavalry to act as his eyes and ears in divining the plans of the Yankees. Before this, General Johnston approved a transfer of a majority of Pemberton's cavalry to

General Bragg in Tennessee. Pemberton retained Wirt Adams's Mississippi cavalry; however, this was not sufficient cavalry given the extensive geographic area to be covered. Pemberton complained bitterly about this loss of cavalry to Johnston, to no avail.

Then followed the defeat of General Bowen at Port Gibson on May 1st. General Pemberton had to retain most of his army in Vicksburg, due to the threat of an attack on Vicksburg from the river, or from the north, where Sherman had one-third of the Federal army. Thus General Bowen had but four brigades to fight four divisions.

From Port Gibson the Yankees turned toward the capital city of Jackson, with McPherson's Corps taking the lead of the Federal army. Confederate General Gregg, with only one brigade, advanced from Jackson to vainly attempt to stop McPherson. This clash occurred near Raymond, Mississippi, and although Gregg's men put up a game fight, they were eventually driven back by overwhelming numbers of Federals.

Grant's army pushed on towards the capital city, at Jackson, Mississippi. General Joe Johnston had about 7,500 men at Jackson. Instead of defending Jackson, behind prepared fortifications that were already in place, Johnston evacuated the capital and, even though he ordered Pemberton to move to Clinton (to join with Johnston's army) and jointly attack the Federals, Johnston inexplicably moved northeast toward Canton, away from Pemberton. The Federals entered Jackson virtually unchallenged, and promptly destroyed manufacturing and military concerns.

General Pemberton had reacted appropriately by sending a brigade each to the various Ferry crossings along the Big Black River. The Big Black constituted a natural barrier between the approaching Federals, and Vicksburg. Those crossings which were defended by the respective Confederate brigades, were at Hankinson's, Halls, and Baldwin's ferries on the Big Black. Orders were also issued to throw up field works at these crossings.

General Pemberton had his chief engineer, Major Lockett, establish field fortifications for the defense of the important points: on the main line of communications at the railroad bridge over the Big Black; and at Edward's Depot.

Correctly deciding that Grant intended to strike the railroad at or near Edward's Depot, and thus cut the Confederates' communications with Jackson, General Pemberton concentrated his "army of maneuver" at Edward's Depot, and near the railroad bridge over the Big Black. This army of maneuver did not include General Forney's and General Smith's divisions, which were left back in the Vicksburg fortifications, in case of direct attack on Vicksburg from the north, or from the river.

The army at Edward's Depot consisted of Bowen's division on the right, Loring's division in the center, and Carter Stevenson's division on the left, in total, about 18,500 men. Some field works had been erected covering all the approaches from the south and east. Had General Pemberton been allowed to wait behind these prepared works and be attacked by General Grant approaching from the east, on ground of Pemberton's own choosing, then that gallant "Pennsylvanian in Gray" might well have been the victor. May 19 and 22, 1863 would show that Grant never could defeat Pemberton's army when Pemberton was defending from behind prepared field works.

In any event, the army remained at Edward's Depot from the 13th to the 15th of May.

During this time General Pemberton had received numerous dispatches from both General Johnston and President Davis. General Johnston said to abandon Vicksburg and move the army to Clinton to meet up with his force. President Davis said to defend Vicksburg. General Pemberton, to harmonize the differing views of Johnston and Davis, marched the three divisions of Bowen, Loring, and Stevenson out from the entrenched works at Edward's Depot, toward Dillon's Plantation, to attack Grant from the rear, while Johnston would engage Grant from the front. The plan might be expressed as a diagram thusly:

Pemberton 18,500 >   Grant 35,000 <   Johnston 6,000
(with Gist and Walker's Brigade's arrival, 9,000

This was not an enviable position for General Grant.

Then, at 7 o'clock a.m. on the morning of the 16th of May, General Pemberton was handed a dispatch from Johnston, telling of the fall of Jackson. Pemberton now knew that Grant's army would be heading back west towards Vicksburg! Thus, General Pemberton reversed the direction of march, and ordered the army to march back to Edward's Depot.

This was perfectly practical and prudent on the part of General Pemberton. General Johnston, in his memoirs written after the war, criticized this decision of Pemberton's as indecisive, and disastrous. This is incorrect. Pemberton's original movement towards Dillon's Plantation was based upon the assumption that the Federal army would be facing toward Jackson. He hoped to march southeast from Edward's Depot and take up a position at Dillon's Plantation, where he would be astride Grant's communication line to Grand Gulf. He would force Grant to attack him in a prepared position. Now, after receiving Johnston's 7 o'clock dispatch, Pemberton realized if he continued his original plan, he would be moving his army outside of its blocking position between Grant and Vicksburg.

About 9 o'clock a.m., Grant's army was making contact with Confederate pickets of Carter Stevenson's division. Stevenson's division bore the brunt of the attack, known to the Confederates as the battle of Baker's Creek, and to the Federals as the battle of Champion Hill.

Bowen and Loring, now actively conspiring to lose a battle so that General Pemberton might be relieved, both refused to obey a direct order from Pemberton to come at once to the aid of Carter Stevenson's division, being destroyed before their very eyes.

This was not the first time General Bowen had shown an inclination to hamper Pemberton, so that Pemberton might be replaced: On the previous night of May 15, Bowen had seen numerous campfires off to the east when he bivouacked that night. This could only portend one ominous thing. Yet Bowen, customarily considered by historians as Pemberton's best division commander, failed to notify Pemberton of this important sight.

Pemberton, when Stevenson's division was being butchered, rode back to try and find the reason for Loring's and Bowen's inactivity. On the way he met Colonel Francis Cockrell and ordered him to bring his Missouri brigade forward to assist General Stevenson's division. Colonel Cockrell, gallant and brave, did not share his division commander's opinion of Pemberton. Cockrell had his brigade ready to attack and was only waiting for the order, so that when Pemberton found him, his Missourians were ready to advance in line of battle. Colonel Cockrell, in a romantic gesture, led the attack with a large Magnolia flower in one hand, and his sword in the other.

Bowen finally came to his senses, perhaps realizing that his actions might very well cost the Confederacy the campaign, and finally brought his remaining brigade (Green's) up, to attack with Cockrell. Bowen's brigade very nearly turned the tide of battle into a Confederate victory. However, Loring's failure to order his division up to the front-line cost Pemberton the battle.

Loring's division was inactive, and Loring even marched it off the field. Instead of retreating to Vicksburg with the rest of Stevenson's and Bowen's divisions, Loring marched it away from Vicksburg, to eventually join Johnston's army north of Jackson. Loring somehow managed to lose a substantial amount of his artillery and supplies during the trek, despite his failure to engage any enemy.

Loring's prior acts of insubordination, regarding his relationships with General R. E. Lee and General "Stonewall" Jackson, in Virginia during 1862, are well known to historians. In fact, Loring's utter contempt for General Jackson nearly caused General Jackson to resign from the army.

It was unfortunate that it was General Stevenson's division who came into contact first with Grant's attacking forces, for although it was numerically the largest of Pemberton's divisions, at around 9000 men, many of its soldiers had never been under fire before this time. Although they put up an initial fight, they were shattered, and began to retreat in a rout. The 56th and 57th Georgia, having never been in a battle, were fleeing back pell-mell, when they reached the Roberts house, where General Pemberton had established a headquarters. General Pemberton himself personally reorganized those two broken regiments, with a speech that, unfortunately, has been lost to history. However, we know its effect served to rally the Georgians, and soon they were fighting alongside of Bowen's division.

Stevenson's and Bowen's division retreated toward the Big Black River Bridge.

The affair of the Big Black Bridge was an attempt of Bowen's division and Vaughn's Tennessee brigade, to halt Grant's approach and hold the road open for Loring's division, who, unbeknownst to Pemberton, would not be coming. Loring, true to form, had never even bothered to send a courier to General Pemberton, advising him as to what he was doing with his division, as he had marched it off the field and out of the battle.

As Major Lockett and General Pemberton watched Vaughn's brigade at the Big Black River Bridge, they saw signs of unsteadiness among the men. When the Federals charged the fortified lines, the Confederate defenders gave way and broke, running away most disgracefully.

General Grant was now able to cross the Big Black and was confident that "one final push" would likewise shatter the Vicksburg line of entrenchments.

However, Grant misjudged the elan of the two remaining divisions (Smith's and Forney's) who had not fought at Champion Hill or Raymond or Port Gibson, and therefore were not demoralized, and who were largely made up of veteran soldiers. These two experienced divisions were placed by General Pemberton to cover the most likely avenues of approach into Vicksburg, such as the Graveyard road, the Jackson road, the Railroad cut, and the Baldwin's Ferry road.

General Grant was confident his troops would easily pierce the Confederate line of fortifications at Vicksburg, as he had won at Raymond, at

or The Maid of Saragoza

Champion Hill and the Big Black River Bridge, and the campaign would be over. In this belief, Grant would be disastrously and horrifically mistaken.

Chapter Eighteen

You have heard that I was incompetent and a traitor — that it was my intention to sell Vicksburg. Follow me and you will see the cost at which I will sell Vicksburg! When the last pound of beef and bacon and flour — the last grain of corn, the last cow and the last man shall perish in the trenches, then and only then will I sell Vicksburg!

— Pemberton To His Men

The Second Texas had been sent with the rest of Moore's Brigade to Snyder's Bluff, guarding the northern approaches to Vicksburg, during the time in late April and early May, that Sherman was making his demonstration, as a feint for Grant's main force crossing the river at Bruinsburg.

On the third of May, the Texan regiment had been ordered to the little town of Warrenton, just south of Vicksburg, where some fortifications blocked the southern approaches to Vicksburg. Here they enjoyed a camping site on a beautiful ridge surrounded by Magnolias which were just beginning to bloom.

The men gathered crawfish by the bag full. William Wiseman, who doubled as a teamster for the brigade, reached his long arms down into the river and brought up a big snapping turtle, which some of the men christened a "first rate dinner," but others would not partake of such a delicacy.

On May 17th, the Second Texas was called from Warrenton to move inside the Vicksburg fortifications. The regiment was aroused from their sleep, at 2 o'clock in the morning, on the night of May 17-18, and exchanged places with the 42nd Alabama regiment, in the lunette on the right of the Baldwin's Ferry road. The 42nd Alabama, after vacating the lunette, was assigned to man the fortifications on the right of the lunette on the Baldwin's Ferry road. In so placing one of his experienced regiments, the Second Texas, in the lunette, General Pemberton correctly gauged the mettle of his veteran regiments and showed great perspicuity in assigning these regiments to key locations on the battlefield. Another instance of this foresight of Pemberton's was his assigning of the Jackson road redan to the battletested Third Louisiana Infantry regiment. Numerous other examples could be cited.

or The Maid of Saragoza

The disposition of the Second Texas regiment, in the lunette on the right of the Baldwin's Ferry road, was as follows: Four companies were in the lunette itself; two companies were in the rifle pits to the right, and the remaining four companies (which included company K), were placed on the left flank, separated by one-hundred yards of space from the lunette itself, and through which passed the Baldwin's Ferry road. The lunette itself was situated on a high knoll commanding the area.

Notwithstanding the fact that the lunette was on a knoll, the Federals were quite fortunate themselves, insofar as several deep valleys debouched (exited) directly in front of the lunette, giving the Federals good cover on their likely avenues of attack.

The Federals also mounted artillery on the hilltops surrounding the lunette, consisting of both heavy siege guns and field batteries, thus ensuring that the lunette would be subject to a fearful battering of shot and shell.

This location (that of the lunette on the right of Baldwin's Ferry road) was the key to this portion of the Confederate works of defense and would be one of the main points of the Federal attack. Despite the gloom from the recent reverses of Stevenson's and Bowen's divisions, at the battle of Baker's Creek, and considering the proximity of the Federals in such overwhelming force, the Second Texas was in excellent spirits. The regiment considered the Vicksburg defenses impregnable and took pride in the thought of defending it during the approaching struggle.

Wright Wiseman and his brother William, and the other young men from Company K were preparing to march out to man the ditch and curtain wall to the left of the lunette. They took one last look over the parapet of the lunette, which was built on the highest ground around, for any sign of movement in their front. One of the sergeants walked up and said that Colonel Moore had ordered the men not to raise any portion of their bodies above the protective walls.

"There will be snipers in the trees," said the sergeant.

"Well dog my cats ef I kin see what tree they may use! Ev'ry tree within nine-mile ha' been cut down by the engineers, an every house has been burned," said William Stayton.

"Them boys that wuz at Baker's Creek must have been badly scared at somethin. Hell-to-split they came over the prairie back towards Vicksburg. Hell-to-split over the prairie! We jes laughed and asked if they hadn't ever had Yankee bullets whizzen around their heads before. An they jes said the 'bullets buzzed like bees, we jes crawled through a fireproof gilt-edged hell!'" laughed Stayton.

"Them boys at Baker's Creek in Stevenson and Lee's divisions were green, they had never seen the elephant before!" said Wright, "like we were before Shiloh."

"How many soldiers you reckon are in front of us this minute?" asked William Wiseman.

"Lord almighty, I seen enuf jes now t' scare hell outta Old Nick and all his imps in Hell! Even without a glass I could see the blue lines o' them Yankee devils just a slinkin' over them hills and hollers into that valley that opens up right in front of us," said Stayton.

"How many?" asked Wright.

"Oh, I judge two brigades, or I am an egg-suckin dawg!" laughed Stayton, "Yessir, sonny, they'll be in yer lap quicker 'an you can say 'Jack Robinson,'" he added.

"The Yankees are moving up artillery also, on all the high ground in our front," said Wright.

Cotton bales had been stacked on top of the Confederate lunette to give it added protection, as the Texans tried to rest before the attack that was sure to come.

Soon the Federal guns were in position and let loose their hellish fury on the lunette and the supporting trenches and curtain wall. Company K had by this time filed off to the left and were now manning the line to the left of the lunette. Cannon had been brought up to strengthen the fortifications which were manned by Company K, although the Confederate artillery was no match for the Federal guns in either number or size.

The bombardment experienced by the Texans in the lunette and the curtain walls on either side of it, was intense in the extreme. Some idea of the number of shells that were fired might be gleaned from the fact that, soon after the bombardment began, a small party was sent out to collect unexploded shells and retrieved two thousand shells near and in rear of the trenches at the lunette, and these were only the ones which had not exploded.

As the Yankees closed in around the lunette, their sharp shooters fired a continual shower of minie balls which rendered it almost certain death for anyone to look over the parapet.

At daylight on Friday the 22nd of May, the Federal artillery opened with unusual ferocity. This could only mean one thing to the Confederates: an assault was imminent.

The night before, Colonel Ashbel Smith, now commanding the regiment, walked along the lines, encouraging the men: "In addition to your Springfield rifles, each man is to have five additional smooth-bore muskets, charged with buckshot, to be used for the close quarters combat," said Colonel Smith.

The artillery barrage was kept up that morning of May 22 until 10 o'clock, when the Federal guns suddenly were quiet, and which was the time for the attack to begin along all the lines. Federal General Benton's and Burbridge's brigades were assigned the task of assaulting the lunette and the curtain wall to its right and left.

Colonel Ashbel Smith was fifty-two years of age and was a physician by training. He owned a splendid plantation "Evergreen" in Harris County, and had personally outfitted the Bayland Guards, a local militia organization, at the outbreak of the war. The Bayland Guards eventually became Company C of the Second Texas, just as the Texana Guards had eventually become Company K. He was fond of classical literature, and during the siege was continually seen in his dugout door, reading his Vergil, even as the shells were bursting overhead. The name by which he was known to one and all was "Old Jingle," referring to the rather ludicrous scene he presented while he awkwardly trotted his horse: his canteen, sword, and spurs making a rattling, clanking noise.

After the Yankee artillery opened at 6 o'clock on the morning of May 22, the Texans in and alongside the lunette on the Baldwin's Ferry road, felt the earth shake and convulse, as if it were a thing of life.

A large valley debouched directly in front of the lunette, thereby shielding the Federals until just before they confronted the Texans. Not long after the Federal guns had fallen silent, one of the Confederate privates in the lunette suddenly shouted, "here they come!" and the Texans raised their heads above the works. They saw the blues lines of soldiers snaking towards the lunette, as if they had sprung from the very bowels of the earth. The Federals were screaming "Vicksburg or hell!" as they approached the glacis of the lunette.

The Texas defenders waited until the Federals had nearly reached the outside wall of the defensive works, before the order was given to "fire." Then a murderous volley was unleashed upon the Federals. Benton's and Burbridge's brigades consisted of five regiments attacking one regiment (the Second Texas), yet, the engineering and placement of the lunette and rifle pits caused it to be a difficult place for the Yankees to capture. The Federals were being killed at a fearful rate, as they tried to climb out of the ditch in front of the lunette and climb into the works. None of the Yankees made it into the lunette, save the color bearer of the 99th Illinois, who was amazingly not hit by a single bullet. Soon the ground in front of the Texans was covered by blue soldiers both dead and dying.

The cannon both in the lunette and along the rifle pits were firing as fast as they could. About 11 o'clock a.m., a cannon exploded near Company K, manning the rifle pits to the left of the lunette. Zach Oppenheimer was killed instantly, Wright Wiseman was seriously injured and taken to the Brigade Hospital behind the lunette. In the same explosion, Abraham Gisler had a leg badly torn, and had to have it amputated. Davey Burnett lost three fingers from his right hand in the incident. The Second Texas had, however, handsomely repulsed the two brigades of the Yankees, capturing a stand of colors from the 99th Illinois, one of the regiments in Benton's brigade.

The Yankees made another attack about 4 o'clock that afternoon on May 22nd. Federal General Sanborn's brigade attempted to flank the lunette on the left. Confederate General Green moved his brigade of Arkansas and Missouri troops to support the Texans, and together they turned back the attack once again, and once more no Yankees were able to pierce the vaunted fortifications at the point where the Baldwin's Ferry road entered the Confederate defenses.

By sunset, the ground around the lunette was littered with so many Federal dead and wounded that a person could have walked in any direction without touching the ground. Major Elliott, of the 33rd Illinois, reckoned that the three Federal brigades making the attacks on the lunette on the Baldwin's Ferry road suffered 600 killed and 1,200 wounded. Be that as it may, there is little dispute that Grant's May 22 attack, which was a massive one, and was made generally along all the lines, was a bloody failure and cost more than 3,000 men in killed, wounded, and missing.

Those soldiers in the lunette were close enough to be able to see Colonel Waul's Texans, who were assisting the Alabamians manning the fort at the railroad cut, make a counterattack to re-take the fort after it had been captured by the Federals. Waul's Texans tossed their lariats over the parapet and pulled down two stands of Yankee colors planted on the parapet of the fort, capturing them as trophies of war.

The Yankees having been thoroughly whipped on May 22nd, finally settled in to conducting a regular siege, keeping up a constant stream of minie balls and cannon shells of all kinds and calibers. The Yankee batteries concentrated their fire on every one of the Confederate artillery pieces that opened on their lines, and quickly dismounted them.

The morning dawned on the 23rd of May, with the same roar of cannon. The Yankee mortar boats on the riverfront continued to throw their tremendous 200-pound shells into the city, coming at the rate of about two per minute. The mortars were wholly inaccurate, and the Yankees

or The Maid of Saragoza

firing them had no idea where in the city they would land. Although the launching of the shells into the city was demoralizing to the civilians, the people endured and defied the Yankees by learning to adapt. Caves were dug by the civilians into the many hills to shelter themselves from the 200-pound shells. They were not as lethal as might be imagined, because it was difficult for the Yanks to ensure that the shell exploded just above the ground, thereby causing the most harm to those under it. The mortars, then, sometimes exploded too high in the air to do damage, and sometimes exploded too low, after they had embedded themselves deep in the ground, where their explosion could do no harm. The speed with which these massive 200-pound mortar shells struck the earth may be illustrated by the statement of Confederate Major Samuel Lockett, who measured the hole in the ground created by one of these mortar shells and found it to be 17 feet deep!

Thus, the mortars were more demoralizing than deadly. At night, the bombardment continued unabated. A monster 15-inch shell crashed down on the Texans in the lunette at the rate of one per minute, not to mention other shells of smaller dimensions. The fragments would fly in every direction, so it was not worthwhile to attempt to dodge them, as one could not tell from what direction they would come from.

During the night of May 24th, the land force of the enemy was quiet. The Confederates speculated that the Federals were working on re-positioning their guns in better positions. The interlude also gave the Confederates the opportunity that night to repair the damage done to their defensive works by the Federal artillery.

At 2 o'clock p.m. on May 25th, a flag of truce was sent to the enemy, requesting them to come and bury their dead. The dead bodies had become so offensive to the Confederates in their trenches, that it became almost impossible for them to stay in them. General Grant agreed to the truce to bury his dead, and remove those still alive, to hospitals. The truce lasted from 6 o'clock until 8 ½ o'clock p.m.

All the Confederates were delighted to have the opportunity to walk and look around without his head being endangered. The Rebs and Yanks were walking, talking, and trading amongst each other.

William Stayton, free to walk about, walked up to the Yankee burial squads:

"Say fellers! Why don't you come in town? Why did you turn back the other evening?... This is the right road to Vicksburg."

Stayton continued to antagonize the Federals, when finally, one Yankee responded to Stayton: "We are gonna give you h__l now, Reb!"

"How you gonna do that, Yank?"

"We're gonna starve you out!" was the frustrated reply.

"Well, when are you coming to pay us another visit?"

Failing to get any further response from the Yankee burial crews, Stayton smiled and pointed at the blue-clad corpses laying in front of the lunette, and said:

"These friends of yours, they didn't make the trip."

About dusk, each side returned to their own works, which were not over two hundred yards apart, in some places, and prepared to resume fighting. It was a very pleasant respite after a constant firing for eight days and nights. That night, Confederate details were organized to rebuild and repair those portions of the works torn down by the fire from the Federal batteries during the day. After fighting in the warm summer sun, the men would labor with pickaxe, shovel and spade, at night, strengthening the ruined breastworks with heavy timbers and cotton-bales.

Chapter Nineteen

> Down upon us heavily runs,
> Silent and sullen, the floating fort,
> Then comes a puff of smoke from her guns,
> And leaps the terrible death,
> With fiery breath,
> From each open port.
>
> — *The Cumberland*

On the 27th of May, the Federal ironclad gunboat *Cincinnati* attacked the upper river batteries. The *Cincinnati* was the most dreaded, most feared, most terrible of all the Federal gunboats. A crowd of spectators had gathered atop "Sky Parlor Hill," a steep eminence located in downtown Vicksburg. Sky Parlor Hill was one of the original hills which had never been reduced to street level by the city fathers, as others had, when the town grew. A footpath led up one side, and steps were built on the other side, to allow for access to the top. Atop the hill stood a little house, occupied by a family.

It was presumed that no Yankee guns or mortars could reach the top of "Sky Parlor," and it was not unusual at all to find curious viewers taking in the scenes of war from the top of this hill. Thus, it was that on that day, May 27, a crowd was gathered on top to watch the duel between the *Cincinnati* and the Confederate river batteries.

The sister of one of the Confederate artillerists manning River battery No. 4, containing the unerring Brooke Rifle cannon, (which had arrived earlier in the year from the Tredegar foundry in Richmond,) had come out, (contrary to orders of General Pemberton for citizens to seek safe shelter), to watch the exchange between the ironclad and her brother's battery. The worried look on her brow evinced her concern for her brother and his comrades.

Suddenly, one of the cannon shots from the *Cincinnati* made a direct hit on the Brooke gun's crew, scattering and temporarily stunning the gunners, but doing no harm to the gun.

Seeing that her brother was wounded, his sister started alone and on foot, toward the battery. She walked along the entrenchments and up to the gun emplacements, as though she had been going to church to show her newest bonnet! Everyone who witnessed this held their breath as they watched the girl calmly approach the battery.

or The Maid of Saragoza

Grabbing the lanyard, she pulled with all her might, to the astonishment of all who were watching. With a roar, the Brooke Rifle belched forth its orange-red tongue of fire, and the white smoke soon enveloped the cannon, as it rocked backwards from the discharge. Lo! The *Cincinnati* is sinking! Whether her magazine was pierced by this shot, or by one from the other river batteries, cannot at this time be accurately determined. It can be positively stated, however, that the citizens and gun crews who witnessed this feat, by a heroine of the siege, soon began to call her the "Maid of Saragoza," recalling those earlier, Napoleonic days, where a poor Spanish girl, in the summer of 1808, arrived on the ramparts of the besieged Spanish city of Saragoza, with a basket of apples for the gunners. She watched the defenders fall to French bayonets. The Spanish troops broke ranks, having suffered heavy casualties, and abandoned their posts. With the French troops a few yards away, the Maid herself ran forward, loaded a cannon, and blasted the attackers at short range. Many a Southerner knew Byron's lines, from Childe Harold:

> Her lover sinks — she sheds no ill-timed tear,
> Her chief is slain — she fills his fatal post,
> Her fellows flee — she checks their base career,
> The foe retires — she heads the sallying host,
> Who can appease like her a lover's ghost?
> Who can avenge so well a leader's fall?
> What maid retrieve when man's flush'd hope is lost?
> Who hangs so fiercely on the flying Gaul,
> Foiled by a woman's hand, before a batter'd wall?

Thus were the exploits of the celebrated Maid of Saragoza, Spain.

The young lady who pulled the lanyard on May the 27th, 1863, in Vicksburg, was Miss Lucy Bertram, originally from the Bluegrass region of Kentucky. She had chosen to follow her brothers in the Confederate army at Vicksburg. Although General Pemberton had, prior to the siege, ordered all civilians to leave Vicksburg, many spurned this order and chose to stay, and among these were Lucy Bertram. She was the guest of a patriotic Vicksburg family who shared their home, victuals, and the cave which had been constructed in the nearby hillside.

The annals of history can furnish no more brilliant record than that of the heroic women of Vicksburg during the Siege of Vicksburg. Regardless of personal danger, they attended to the brave, wounded and dying defenders.

Thus began the Siege of Vicksburg, forever enshrining these four words in the annals of history. The courageous, heroic display of manliness and fortitude have made the entrenchments surrounding Vicksburg hallowed ground forever, and the deeds performed and privations suffered, an ever-popular theme for the poets and chroniclers of America.

Chapter Twenty

A life on the Vicksburg Hills, a home in the trenches deep,
A dodge from the Yankee shells, and the old pea bread won't keep.
Like a Rebel caged I pine, and I dodge when the cannon roar,
But give me corn dodgers and swine and I'll stay forevermore.
— *A Life On The Vicksburg Hills*

The large number of items from the sunken *Cincinnati*, picked up on the river, were curious and interesting to the defenders and citizenry of Vicksburg.

By far the most intriguing was a doctor's medical chest containing a letter being written to his wife. Amidst the hay, clothing, whiskey and photographs found floating near the sunken hulk, this missive from a Federal surgeon, which never reached its intended destination, was passed around Confederate hands, to be perused and studied.

The Indiana surgeon told his wife that the *Cincinnati* had been given the express mission of destroying the upper river batteries, and that General Sherman would march into the City of Vicksburg "before sunset." The surgeon mentioned that the *Cincinnati* had also been given the dual mission of silencing the famous Confederate gun, "Whistling Dick," which had been emplaced in various positions, along the river batteries of Vicksburg. The cannon was an 18-pounder siege and garrison weapon, based on the pattern of 1839, and which had been converted from smoothbore to rifled bore. This gun had been made famous and drew the attention of newspaper correspondents for northern papers.

One newspaper correspondent, who was covering the war for the readers back in Ohio, was briefing another reporter who was writing stories for his paper in New York:

"The rebels have a gun which domineers the river and is a pestilent bother to us. They call him 'Whistling Dick.' No gunboat has any business where this terrible gun can get a shot at it. It shoots a ball two and one-half feet long, steel pointed, weighing two hundred and fifty pounds, can tear through our best iron-clads, and is thought to be the best gun of the war." **Note C. Whistling Dick.**

"Where is he emplaced?" asked the other reporter.

"Oh, that's just it. Infernal thing moves around. Earlier this year, Whistling Dick had been trained toward the canal being dug by Grant, across from the south end of the river batteries, and was making some good shots. Needless to say, 'Dick' impeded our progress on the canal."

"And the name? Where does that come from?"

"The name comes from the fact that the gun is distinguishable from all other Rebel weapons of defense by the noise with which it announces its presence and mission. The noise made by the projectile is a tremendous whiz … as if all the imps in the infernal regions were practicing phonetics on the final letter of the alphabet."

"Pray tell what could cause such a whistling noise? Could the type of projectile account for this strange effect?"

"Some think that the projectile is a solid shot, shaped somewhat like an auger, and intended to pierce iron-clad vessels. I suppose that could account for the sound. It is also supposed that when the Confederates were cutting the rifling grooves in the tube, that some imperfection resulted in the shell leaving the gun with a peculiar whistling sound."

"What has the Federal Navy done to address this?"

"Oh, they have certainly tried to take him out, and have only succeeded with knocking him off his carriage. Anyone who is fired at by this gun, does not soon forget the experience, and even if the projectile does not find the target, the intended victim is generally scared out of his wits by the sound," concluded the discussion between the two reporters.

Not only did the ironclad *Cincinnati* fail to disable the celebrated "Whistling Dick," but "Dick" in fact materially contributed to the sinking of the *Cincinnati* on that day, having registered several lethal hits.

Chapter Twenty-One

> T'was at the siege of Vicksburg, of Vicksburg
> of Vicksburg, of Vicksburg —
> T'was at the siege of Vicksburg,
> When the Parrott shells were whistling through the air.
> —*The Siege Of Vicksburg* (to the air of the *"Listen to the Mockingbird"*)

The hospital ward in which Wright Wiseman lay wounded, was where Miss Lucy Bertram, whose heroics had been proclaimed all throughout the city and along the lines, was serving as a nurse. She was occasionally queried about the notoriety that had occurred at the river battery, however, modestly preferred not to speak of the cannon firing incident. Her presence in the hospital ward was noticed, and persons would whisper up and down the ward: "That is her, see her calm and pretty face, ministering to the other wounded soldiers."

Miss Bertram would, in addition to her nurse duties, swat away flies and read to the suffering patients in the hospital from the small library located there, to pass the long hours. Hesiod's Theogony was a popular volume. One of the favorite stories was that of the love story of the god Cupid and the mortal girl Psyche.

"Psyche was the youngest and prettiest of three sisters. Her beauty was almost supernatural. Venus, who was jealous of Psyche, turned to Cupid, asking him to make the girl fall in love with a man from a low station. But Cupid fell in love with Psyche. He took her to his palace, which he visited only at nightfall. He prevailed upon the girl not to try to discover his identity, or he would leave her," read Miss Bertram.

"One night," Miss Bertram continued, "the curious Psyche lit an oil lamp to see the face of her beloved. A drop of hot oil fell on Cupid and he awoke and fled from Psyche angrily.

"Psyche searched the world over for Cupid. Venus, still in a jealous mood, subjected her to several trials that Psyche was able to overcome only with divine intervention. Cupid at length, regretted his actions and longed for Psyche, eventually he found her, and requested that Jupiter transform her from a mortal to the embodiment of a goddess. Then the newly minted goddess and Cupid were wedded," concluded Miss Bertram.

Especially popular with the hospital invalids was the recitation of the beautiful little poem *"Ode to Psyche,"* in which the poet, (Keats), pays respectful homage to the goddess, Psyche. The poet, pledges to worship her, and concludes his poem, in remembering that Cupid visited Psyche only in the dark of night, with the promise to love her and to carry:

> A bright torch, and a casement ope at night,
> To let the warm love in!

Whenever Miss Bertram entered the hospital ward, she was greeted with the request: "Miss Bertram, read to us from your book!" and "Miss Bertram, sit down beside me and read to me."

On this day, May 28, was a very sad day for the boys from Jackson County. The cannon explosion of May 22nd had wrought horrible wounds to Wright Wiseman, his one arm having been mangled, and several severe wounds to the lower abdomen, were clear. The patch work efforts of the physicians to save his life, were also evident. Miss Bertram was fanning Wright. His brother William, Davey Burnett, Frankie Burwell, William Stayton, and the ever-faithful Ben, Wright's body servant, were all present.

"Doctor, how long have I to live?"

"A very few hours."

"Oh, my dear mother! Quick, I want to write."

With a shaky hand, he wrote:

My dear mother,

This is the last you may ever hear from me. I have time to tell you that I died like a man, and we repulsed the enemy, and our trenches were stained with the blood of the Yankees. Bear my loss as best you can. Remember that I am true to my country and my greatest regret at dying is that she is not free and that you and my brothers and sister are robbed of my worth, whatever that may be. I hope that this will reach you and you must not regret that my body cannot be recovered. I cannot write more.

Nathaniel Wright Wiseman
Company K
2nd Texas

This letter was given to Lucy Bertram to give to his mother.

Wright asked: "Doctor, I am in great agony, can you give me anything to alleviate the pain?"

Whereupon a cup of a concentrated dose of opium was handed to him to drink. Wright feebly waved the cup, saying:

"Come around, boys, and let us have a toast. I drink the toast to you to the Southern Confederacy and to victory!"

There was not a dry eye amongst these now hardened veteran soldiers. In a few minutes he was sleeping painlessly.

"He is sleeping now," said Miss Bertram to his brother, "he has passed in and out of consciousness. During a lucid moment he told me about how he wants to go back home to his horses and cattle in Texas, but that he had a feeling that he would never again lay eyes upon them. He told me to take his memorandum book, and his watch, and to see that they were returned to his mother in Texas, if he did not make it back. He said he had a sweetheart waiting for him back in Texas, and asked me to deliver some poetical effusions he had composed, but had never given, to her before he left:

To Miss ----------:

>A Texas boy now bids a long farewell,
>To one whose kindness like a light has shone
>Upon his dreary hours; whose voice a spell
>Has woke the memory of days now gone.
>A star he'll bear along the front of battle,
>Where foe, meets foe mid-carnage and mid strife.
>Perchance amongst bursting bomb and cannons rattle
>He'll yield that star, but only with his life.
>But should a bright & happier lot prevail,
>Returned to home & all that he holds dear,
>He'll wear that star, a pledge that ne'er can fail,
>To show thy kindness to the volunteer."

"He was named for a poet," said his brother William, "he wrote some poetry back home, too, but I do not think he had a girl waiting. He had one once, but that was long ago, and that poem could not have been referring to her. He was always interested in music and paintings and had a strong imagination and was an artist of rare ability."

The other soldiers said their goodbyes and squeezed his hand and tried to keep up a brave face. After they had left the hospital ward, Lucy Bertram sat next to his cot, as did his brother. Wright intently read their solemn faces but spoke not. The doctor walked up and told his brother that the medicines and surgery had failed to produce the desired effect. Gradually, the calmness of death came over Wright as he slowly closed his eyes, and he appeared to drift back to that eventful day, May the 22nd, speaking some audible words: "here they come! ... pick your targets, boys

… aim low … there he is! … get him! … they keep coming … there … there." And then his words became garbled and incoherent. Eventually death came to close this extraordinary boy's life. The tears streamed down Miss Bertram's face.

Wright's brother and Miss Bertram wanted to have a proper funeral with burial in the city cemetery, but the doctors would not consent to it, saying "all soldiers were worthy of attention," and that no distinction should be allowed. So, before he was buried in a trench grave dug in the yard beside the Brigade hospital, behind the lunette that Wright and his compatriots had so nobly defended, Miss Bertram clipped a lock of his hair, and dutifully promised to faithfully transmit the precious lock and his few personal effects to his old mother, Sarah Wiseman, waiting back home in Texas.

Chapter Twenty-two

Here, 'neath the giant hills,
Rest warriors, rest ye!
Lulled by the murm'ring rills,
None shall molest ye!
Fanned by our south wind's breath,
Sleep soldiers weary!

— Dedication At Vicksburg

By the last days of May, the Rebels were beginning to be physically worn down by the unusually warm weather, the constant sharpshooting and cannonading of the enemy, and the never ceasing night work in repairing the earthwork fortifications. The men's sleep was disturbed by the continuous heavy cannonading. The siege now extending into the month of June, the rationing of food caused the defenders to be much reduced in flesh. Now, a mixture of ground peas and meal were issued as the main staple of the men's diet. This food was unhealthy, as the pea flour and meal did not cook at the same rate. Consequently, it was almost impossible to thoroughly bake both pea flour and meal equally, such that one half would inevitably remain undercooked, and therefore unfit for consumption.

During the entire siege, the city and fortifications were rife with rumors that General Joe Johnston was marching toward Vicksburg to succor the garrison. Almost daily, his cannons could be heard in the direction of the Big Black! Alas, these rumors and sounds were but apparitions!

The cannonading of the enemy on the morning of the 29th of May was the most terrific yet experienced. Fortunately, little damage was done, one man was lost, and one Negro was killed. The day passed quietly away until 5 o'clock p.m., when the scene of the morning was re-created with terrible ferocity.

On Saturday May 30th, Company K lost another three of its soldiers. A shell exploded overhead and killed William Sims, Eli O'Berry and L. G. Thermon. There were five O'Berry brothers who joined the Second Texas at the commencement of the war, now only one was left still alive, and ere the war was over, he too would be killed!

Most wounds experienced by the Confederates were head wounds, as that was the part of the body most exposed above the breastworks.

or The Maid of Saragoza

It was a common occurrence, at about 3 o'clock in the morning, for the Yankee land batteries to open with all their might and ferocity. It was truly a grand spectacle to see and experience. The sounds from the shells were anything but pleasant. Some made a screeching sound and others a most melancholy moaning sound. The soldiers were still busy digging caves in the banks of earth so that they may escape the shells while sleeping. The enemy failed to make any assaults following these artillery barrages, they having despaired of taking the place by storm, and being determined to starve out and to wear out the Confederates, by not allowing any rest or repose.

The Federal mortar shells, which were 15- and 18- inch diameter, and weighed two hundred and fifty pounds, were filled with small pieces of iron, and would usually burst in the air and scatter their contents in every direction. During the night, fifty of these monsters would be fired at Rebel positions, the men having taken to their "holes." When they would explode, the earth would shake, reminiscent of an earthquake.

Sterling Fisher of the Second Texas, was badly wounded, on June 2, by the explosion of a shell, and was taken to the hospital. He was not expected to survive his wounding. His right leg was amputated just above the ankle, and he was cut on his back near the shoulder blade, and on his buttocks.

Sterling stood his wounds like a soldier and believed he would recover. The Confederates had no nourishing food with which to feed the wounded, and consequently, their wounds would not heal properly. The meals consisted of the familiar peas and meal, which was not a very palatable diet. On occasion the soldiers were served what was purported to be fresh beef. Some said it was mule meat, and it may have been, but to many there was no great difference that could be detected.

The enemy sapping in the ground was now approaching the salient of the lunette at the right of the Baldwin's Ferry road, with a sap-roller, which is a great roller made of withers and saplings about six feet long and four feet high. The sap-roller is pushed along in front of the sappers, who are digging a trench running up to the face of the fortifications. These "approaches," were often in a "zig-zag" design. Once the approaches had gotten close enough, the Federals would construct "parallels," which were trenches that ran parallel to the Confederate line, and ever so closer to their earthworks.

The days passed…still no word of General Joe Johnston and the relief army. General Johnston was sent reinforcements, numbering some 30,000 troops, and was ordered by the government, through Secretary of

War Seddon, to attack Grant's rear, and attempt to raise the siege.

Vicksburg "must not be lost without a struggle," he wrote Johnston, the "honor and interests of the Confederacy demand it." The risk was assumed by Secretary Seddon — taken even from Johnston's shoulders — yet Johnston still would not budge. For some forty days, Johnston not only failed to move toward Vicksburg, but he had also taken no steps to reconnoiter the geographical landscape, or plan how best to approach.

Meanwhile, the Confederates in the trenches passed the dreary hours away. They were told to conserve ammunition and not to fire upon the enemy unless the enemy launched an assault. The Confederate artillery rarely responded to the Federal artillery, for the same reasons. This policy engendered some resentment on the part of the men, as might be expected, but General Pemberton was again correct: it was unknown how long the siege would last, and therefore prudence dictated the conservation of ammunition.

On Sunday June 14, brave Lieutenant Kirk of Company K was killed by a piece of exploding shell.

The Brigade commissary was asked by a neighboring lady, a Mrs. Holt, to "for God's sake, send her a peck of meal and some peas," that she had laid back a six months' supply, but that her house and all she had, had been burnt. It was at Mrs. Holt's house that Lt. Colonel Timmons had been cared for, after his wounding at Chickasaw Bayou, in December 1862, and later died there. This gave the Confederates great pleasure to think that they could help this lady, and the requested articles were sent.

On June 16th, a courier, after having laid in a swamp for the better part of two weeks, arrived with 200,000 percussion caps, a most needed article.

William Stayton, although considered one of the very flower of Southern chivalry, was nevertheless a very indifferent reader and even a more indifferent speller, and he walked, bent over as all the Texans had to walk while in their works, holding a piece of paper in his one hand, while searching for the better-read one-legged commissary Major, Maurice Simons.

"It's hotter than forty hells in here. ... Major Simons where air you?" shouted Stayton.

"Over here, Stayton, in my hole."

Stayton handed the paper he held to the Commissary Major, who was escaping the rays of the sun by lying in his little hole dug into a wall of the fortification: "Major, read this here letter would you please, afore I send it on its way?"

or The Maid of Saragoza

" I will read it, but you know we have no way of getting letters out. I have been keeping a journal for my Lizzie. But I will read your letter."

"I warn you I am an indifferent speller, for I was absent on the day we studied grammar," said the tall, handsome Stayton with a smile.

"One of the blessings of having a good wife like Lizzie, she has encouraged me to read widely," said the Major.

We furnish the reader with the text of Stayton's letter, with all its original spellings:

To Miss Mary -------------
   In the beseiged City of Vicksburg June 20, 1863
   in the glorious rein of Jeff. Davis

Dear Mary,

I write you a fiew lines to let you know that I am fine and am still in the bullpen here at Vicksburg.

I will try to send this letter threw the lines with the help of some Yankey Missourians that we occasionally trade tobaacy with.

Miss Mary remember me to Miss Emma and all the ladys of the two Kronkawas who sent us clothing by way of Col. Smith. If you see John Miller tell him I am well and killing all the Yankeys that lays in my power. Don't show this one if you pleas for I don't want the Union people to find out that as soon as I can get a furlow we are coming back to surprise & I will bring plenty of men to clean up all the Yankeys that is at Texana and along the two Kronkawas.

I am living now to avenge the lives of many a Jackson County boy that have given up their lives for the great and loved Country of the Southern Confederacy so by the grace of god if am killed I die in a good cause.

(Signed) Private Wm. Stayton
Co. "K"
2d Texas Volunteers

"Son, I pronounce your letter one of rare artistic beauty, I would not change a line," said the Commissary Major as he handed the letter back to Stayton.

"Good, now let's get it to those Alabamians, who meet up with those Missouri Yankees, every night at the "Trysting place", and lets git that letter on its way," said Stayton.

A unique feature of the War Between the States was the inclination of the private soldiers to fight with ferocity during the day, yet to engage in fraternization with each other at night or during lulls in the fighting. Swapping Northern coffee for Southern tobacco was a commonplace picket activity. To prevent surprise attacks, both armies posted pickets in advance of their lines at night. With the lines so close in the latter stages of the siege, pickets would often stand within a few feet of one another.

That evening, some of the pickets yelled over to the other side:
"Hello Yank!"
"Hello Johnnie!"
"How did you enjoy the day?"
"Fine! How do you like your mule meat?"
"It is sweet and savory, Yank. How do you like your hardtack? The hardtack you sent over yesterday was so hard we could not chew it!"
(Laughter)…"Say, Reb, do you have any tobaccy?"
"Yes, we have some. We have some letters. Will you see that they get mailed?"
"Where so they need to go?"
" The part of Texas occupied by your army."
" If you send some tobaccy over with it, we will see that your mail gets through the lines."

And so, another night closed on the siege of Vicksburg, with the pickets taking matters into their own hands, despite their superior's strictures about fraternization.

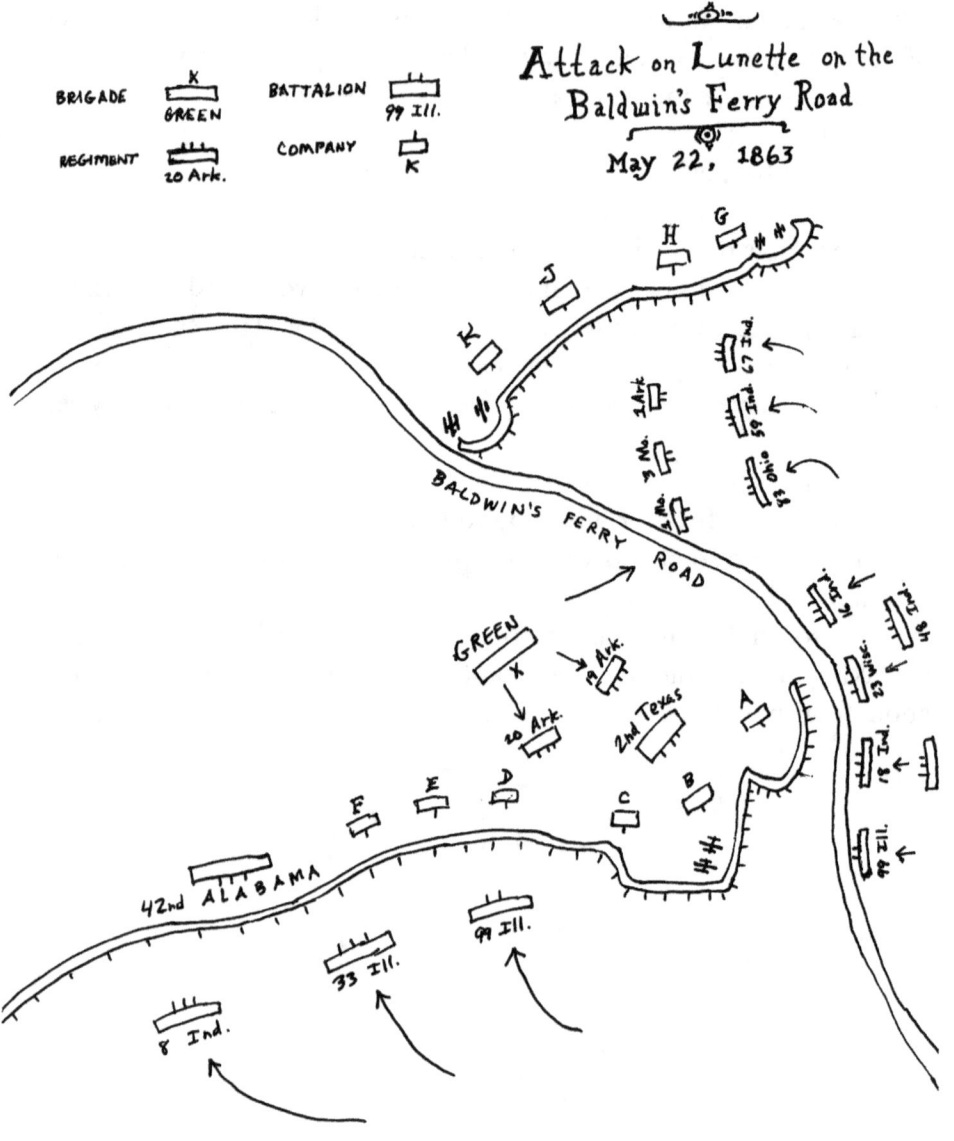

Chapter Twenty-three

> AMONG the dwellings framed by birds
> In field or forest with nice care,
> Is none that with the little Wren's
> In snugness may compare. ...
> There to the brooding bird her mate
> Warbles by fits his low clear song,
> And by the busy streamlet both
> Are sung to all day long.
>
> — *A Wren's Nest*

One of the incidents of the siege that amused the Texans in their fort, and alleviated their boredom and strain, was the presence of an energetic little brown wren. Wrens, who unlike all other members of North American birds, prefer to reside in objects made by man, rather than nests made by themselves, or an object furnished by nature. This trait renders them one of the most sociable of the feathered tribe. But there was much about these tiny brown birds to admire in addition to this.

There was an old metal can that had been discarded and was laying on top of one of the huge cotton bales used to fashion the traverses dividing the lunette's gun emplacements. A wren began building a nest in this can, and thus this little bird set up housekeeping amidst the heroic scenes of human strife and struggling. However, his presence had an ameliorating effect on all who were amused by the antic behavior of this diminutive comedian.

His incessant singing of his delightful song was a feature of courtship, inviting his ladylove to reside with him in his humble castle he had so proudly filled with sticks and an assortment of colorful nesting material, such as bright shiny pieces of paper or discarded clothing.

Soon he had attracted the female, and before long they were raising their young charges. These little brown birds created an intriguing fascination, with their constant going and coming with flitting upcocked tails, their innumerable visits to the nest with food to satisfy their clamoring young, their chattering vibrant songs, and their saucy scolding when a soldier ventured too nearby. For all these reasons, the pair of wrens gained countless human friends, who cherished the presence of these birds, both as a reminder that God's natural world was still near, and for their example of fortitude, amidst the shells and minie balls of Man, during the mighty Siege of Vicksburg.

By June 17th, the enemy sap-rollers were within twenty yards of the lunette. Their working party was not visible, having entered the ground at the bottom of the valley in front of the lunette, and by digging deep, could not be fired at as they approached the lunette. The Federals were now tunneling under the lunette, to undermine it. The Rebels in response to this, cut a deep ditch in the rear of the lunette, to attempt to intercept the Federal tunnel.

The Confederate engineer in charge had been ordered to place thundering barrels (filled with gunpowder) to roll down the attacking Yankees, and loaded shells with short-time fuses, as preparations for meeting assaults. This was done at all the Confederate principal forts, by the engineers in charge. Thus, the Confederates were preparing a very warm welcome for the next time the Yankees visited in town.

The enemy made better progress at the redan guarding the Jackson road, garrisoned by the Third Louisiana. On the 25th of June, the enemy exploded a small mine under the fort, tearing off the vortex of the Third Louisiana Fort. The Fort was stormed, but the Yankees were handsomely repulsed.

On the 1st of July, the enemy again exploded a mine under the Third Louisiana Fort, and this time the charge of gunpowder was truly massive, a Federal engineer later told the Confederates one and a quarter tons were used. This second mine explosion virtually destroyed the fort, but no assault was made this second time. Instead, for six hours, two 9-inch Dahlgren guns, a battery of large Parrotts, a field-gun battery, and a Coehorn mortar unleashed a most hellish barrage of projectiles against the Rebel fort.

Despite the daring exploits of Lamar Fontaine, Captain Saunders, and courier Walker, who floated down the river on logs and brought, inside the lines, respectively 18,000, 20,000, and 200,000 caps, the Confederates were running out of ammunition. Additionally, provisions had been reduced to quarter rations. Since there were not enough men in the trenches to allow for sufficient rest, the men were, by July 2, exhausted to the point that they were only fit for simple standing in the trenches and firing. The lines were battered, and many guns were dismounted.

The Confederates nevertheless had prepared to stop the Yankees a third time. The Rebel engineers had eleven mines containing from 100 to 125 pounds of gunpowder, ready to be fired as of July 1. Galleries (underground shafts) had been dug by the Confederates, extending eight feet deep, and twenty feet in front of the works, with fuses set, waiting for the approach of the Federal sappers.

General Pemberton called a council of war, on the 2nd of July, at his headquarters on Crawford Street. He began by stating he had given up all hope of General Johnston ever relieving the garrison. All present, except for the gallant Generals S. D. Lee and Baldwin, voted to surrender. Pemberton said he concurred in the near unanimous decision, but that it would be: "Far better for me to die at the head of my troops, while leading a desperate attempt to cut our way out, than the obloquy which I know will be heaped upon me. But my duty is to sacrifice myself to save the army which has so nobly done its duty to defend Vicksburg."

The decision to surrender on the 4th of July was not well received with many in the Confederacy, and only served to confirm in the minds of many Southerners, the perfidy of General Pemberton, a native Northerner. However, he was able to obtain very generous terms from General Grant on account of it. As a result of the favorable terms Pemberton was able to extract from Grant, his soldiers were spared from being sent to the Northern prisoner of war camps, just as bad for the Confederates, (although not as well known), as Andersonville was for the Yankees.

On May 2nd, when the Second Texas had left their camp at Chickasaw Bayou, without a change of clothes and one blanket to a man, they fought uncomplainingly, under constant rifle fire and frequent heavy cannonading, and incessant mental strain on account of the enemy's steady approach, from May 17 to July 4th. When it rained, they slept in the mud; when the sun burned them, they endured. They used water from shallow wells and had daily rations of three ounces of musty cornmeal and pea flour. Yet when they were surrendered, they wept.

Chapter Twenty-four

I'll save myself thro' the dead struggle,
And when the great battle is o'er
I'll claim my full rations of laurels,
As always I've done heretofore.
I'll swear that I fought them as bravely
As the best of my comrades who fell —
And swear to all others around me,
That I never had fears of a shell.
— *Do They Miss Me In The Trenches?*

Upon the capitulation of Vicksburg on July 4th, the Confederates could march out of the lines, upon the signing of paroles not to take up arms again, until properly exchanged. The Confederacy granted leave for the men to return home to Texas to see their families. Thus, within a short time, the city was emptied of Rebel soldiers, except those too sick to be moved. Sterling Fisher, still ailing in the Brigade hospital, fell into this category. Poor conditions and lack of nutritious food caused him to slowly decline.

A Federal soldier entered the tent of one of the hospitals, his step betraying a noticeable limp. He stopped and looked around as if he were looking for someone or something.

"Are there any of the Second Texas Infantry here?" asked the Federal.

"Yes" replied one of the sick soldiers, pointing to Sterling.

The Yankee approached Sterling and asked, "Do you belong to the Second Texas Infantry?"

"I do."

"Were you in the battle of Shiloh?"

"I was."

"Did your regiment wear white negro cloth clothes in that battle?"

"It did."

The Yankee drew a worn memorandum book from his pocket and thrust it towards Sterling.

"Do you know the men whose names are written there?"

Focusing the best he could, Sterling said: "I do; the first name is mine, the other is Davey Burnett's."

The Yankee's lips quivered, his body trembled, his eyes moistened, and with a husky voice, asked:

"Do you know me?"

"I do not."

"Did you write that?"

"That is my hand-writing."

"Do you remember picking up three men and putting them on a bed of leaves in the shade, and giving them water and something to eat, and taking a watch off the captain and putting it in his pocket, and putting them in an ambulance, and sending them to the hospital?"

"Yes."

"I'm one of them," said the Yankee as tears flowed down his cheek.

"You saved my life and that of my captain and comrade, and I have hunted for you or some of your command on every battlefield since, that I might prove myself true to you; now, what can I do for you?"

"Nothing," replied Sterling.

"But I must do something. Do you need money? (he held out his well-filled purse) You must, for you are in our lines now and your money is worthless."

"No, I have plenty of money, gold and silver, given me by my comrades when they left me."

"Well, you will need clothing?"

"No, I cannot sit up; and have no need of clothes until I am able to be up, which will be many months yet."

"Tell me how you are wounded."

Sterling told how he had been wounded by three pieces of a shell; how the hospital being only supplied with one nurse to ten patients they could not give the patients proper attention; how in spite of their best efforts the maggot–fly would light on every damp spot on bed or clothing, leaving numerous almost microscopic maggots, which would find lodgment in any crease of the skin, and eat its way into the flesh; and had eaten between his helpless fingers, behind his ears, and in the creases of his neck; how with the demands of three large wounds to feed, his system had cried for food and had struggled with starvation; how his bones at knee and hip had cut through the skin, and for more than a month he had been compelled to lie on these, burning with the fires of torment, because he could lie in no other position; how he had never been dejected or cast down until the surrender, and all his friends had gone out from him, and with them all hope for the cause for which he had proudly suffered.

"Are the surgeon's kind to you?" asked the Federal.

"I have not seen one for quite some time."

"I will tell them who you are and what you did for me. How strange it is that we should meet again with our circumstances so reversed! I have never forgotten your kindness or your face, but you look so young — so much like a mere boy. You were a man when we met each other at Shiloh."

"Yes, I have lost my hair and beard since I was wounded; all came out, and this new short hair and beard makes me look young."

"But you need better food than you get here. I must bring in some of our officers and tell them who you are, and hereafter you will be well treated; I know you will."

He then disappeared, but reappeared an hour later, with the Federal surgeon in charge of all the hospitals in the town, to whom this strange tale of another day was told. The Federal surgeon surveyed Sterling's situation, examined his person and wounds, and asked many questions of the staff charged with his immediate care. He was singularly unimpressed.

"Why have these bedsheets not been changed?" asked the surgeon.

"He is dying," came the reply from the Yankee orderly.

"And what is this contemptible concoction you are serving him?" came the next question.

"It is better than he was getting before the surrender," said the orderly, "we are using the fresh food for our sick and wounded, there is not enough for the Rebels."

"And why has this man's wounds not been cleaned and dressed properly?" continued the surgeon, his aggravation at the answers being given by the orderly steadily increasing.

"We can only do so much. There are not sufficient staff with which to attend to all of the Rebels, Colonel."

The Federal surgeon turned to his staff officers who were trailing behind him, and made the following remarks:

"I want fresh fruit and vegetables brought down immediately. Clean linen, including pillow sheets and blankets, will be put on his bed. This gruel ..." (which he picked up off of Sterling's bed and contemptuously flung out an open window) "is not fit for animal consumption, much less human. The staff here are permanently relieved. Bring my personal staff, including nurses, to attend the men in this ward, and specifically, to this Texan ... move!"

The orderlies and nurses who had previously had charge of Sterling slinked sheepishly away, and a new set of doctors, nurses and orderlies were brought in.

Thus, Sterling Fisher obtained a new lease on life, as it were, and not only lived for the next day, but lived to return to green pastures of coastal

or The Maid of Saragoza

Texas once again, thanks in part to the grace of God, and in part to the beneficence of the Yankee medical officer, and his Yankee friend from the battlefield of Shiloh. **Note D. Sterling Fisher.**

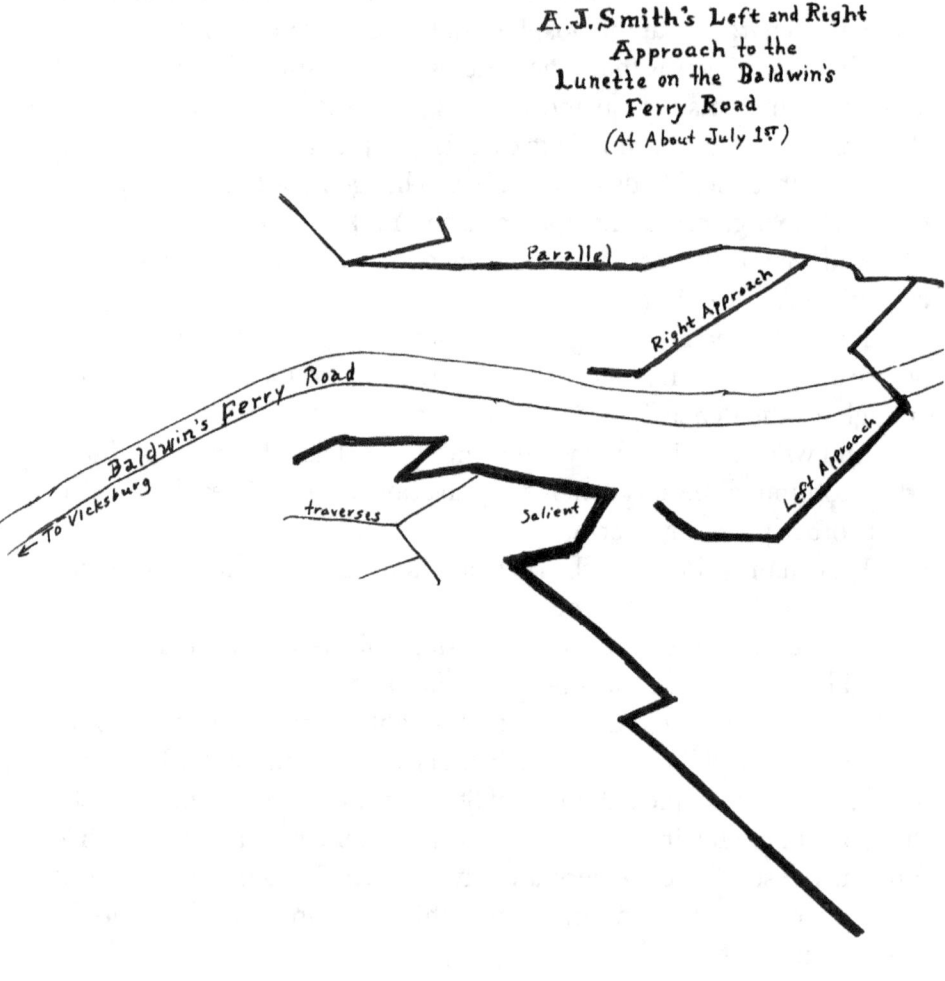

Chapter Twenty-Five

We have received reports that Vicksburg has capitulated, although we do not credit these reports. ...
The fall of the Confederate Gibraltar! The Confederacy split in twain! The thought is too awful to contemplate!
— *Richmond Examiner*, July 10, 1863

The Confederates had fought the Federals to a standstill, and the Federals acknowledged that Pemberton's lines at Vicksburg were impossible to break, no matter how many men they had on hand.

The only way to conquer was to starve the garrison out. Johnston had defied direct orders from Richmond to raise the siege, and although he moved his army toward Vicksburg, had remained idle too long, and while Johnston was idle, the Federals had amassed a huge army surrounding Vicksburg. Thus, the capitulation of Vicksburg had taken place.

By the terms of surrender that had been agreed to between Generals Pemberton and Grant, as soon as the rolls could be made out, and paroles signed by officers and men, the Confederates would be allowed to march out of their lines, the officers taking with them their side-arms and clothing, and the rank and file allowed their clothing but no other property.

The Negro servants still serving in the army, were expressly prohibited from passing through the lines with their masters. These prohibitions had circulated amongst the soldiers the night before the surrender, and William Wiseman had thought the matter over. He stood in the line to be passed outside the lines to go to the paroled prisoners camp at Enterprise, Mississippi. The Yankee soldier in charge told William that he could pass, but that Ben his servant would not be allowed to go with him.

"Ben has been with me through the entire war, ever since May of '61. He and I and my brothers have grown up together these last several years, can you make an exception?" asked William.

"No, I cannot."

"Sergeant, look at it from my perspective," pleaded William, "Ben has never had to look out for himself, he has always had me or my brother to assist him, just as he has assisted me with cooking and soldiering. If you cast him out to fend for his self, is it not a cruelty and an injustice to him, without any preparations for the trials of life?"

William tried his best to persuade the Yankee sergeant, but to no avail. Finally, William turned to Ben, and said:

"Now Ben (dry your eyes, do not let the Yankees see your tears). Here is one hundred dollars in gold pieces, I have saved, you take these (do not let anyone take these from you) use it to pay for your food and lodging and any expenses for the journey back to Texas. Save some and use it to buy a horse when you can. Remember to save some money for the river crossings. Buy a suit of clothes. Lastly, and importantly, here is a piece of paper. I have decided that to keep you from being detained as a runaway, it would be best to give you your freedom, that's what these papers are, Ben, I have signed my name to this letter, granting you a free man. Now, don't you cry, Ben. God keep you."

The two young men embraced, and Ben could hardly speak:

"Ah will tell Miss Sarah 'bout Wright, when ah git home."

The Federal sergeant tried to grab the emancipation documents out of Ben's hand, saying:

"These are important, let me read them to you …" he started to say.

William snatched the papers out of the sergeant's grip, and returned them to Ben, with the terse words for the Yankee:

"He can read them. We taught him to read. I will thank you not to bother him any more than you already have," and the two young men parted, one going back to Texas, the other to the paroled prisoner camp.

The regimental flag of the Second Texas mysteriously disappeared, and despite the assiduousness of the Yankees to locate it, nothing was ever found. It was commonly assumed that the regimental flag had been torn into shreds and distributed, or wholly destroyed, to prevent capture.

Miss Bertram, waiting with the other civilians to pass out of the lines, had in fact concealed the flag in the folds of her dress, and the Yankee officer in charge of searching those persons passing through the lines, was shamed by Miss Bertram into non-action:

"I presume you as a gentleman will accept my word of honor that I am not concealing any contraband, or will you reinforce the notion that some of my people have, as to the notorious and base nature of all Yankees?" said Miss Bertram.

"Miss Bertram, I am a gentleman who holds no unkind feelings for your people. I have never laid my hands upon a lady, and do not intend to start now. If you give me your word, you may pass through the lines," said the Yankee.

"Then you give me hope that we are mistaken about the Yankee character, and that one day our peoples may co-exist peacefully, after we have secured our independence, of course," replied Miss Bertram.

The Yankee merely smiled and allowed Miss Bertram to proceed, and no one was the wiser concerning the whereabouts of the flag of the Second Texas.

Her next effort was to prepare for the passage to Texas, to make good on her promise to return Wright's effects to his mother. She was advised to travel to New Orleans, and there would be put into contact with a blockade runner who could put her safely on the Texas coast. However, there being no mode of transportation to New Orleans, she turned to her newfound Texas friends.

Chapter Twenty-Six

Daughters of Southland! Come bring ye bright flowers,
   Weave ye a chaplet for the brow of the brave,
Bring ye the emblems of freedom and victory,
   Bring ye the emblems of death and the grave …
— Rode's Brigade

William Wiseman, the mute Davey Burnett, William Stayton, and the one-legged commissary officer, Major Maurice Simons, having reported to the paroled prisoner camp, after about a month secured their leaves to return to Texas. The soldiers agreed to act as the "escort" for Miss Bertram's journey to Jackson County, and wagons were hired to carry the extra travelers. The Texans were of course anxious to see how their families were faring, since mail service had been completely cut off during the siege, and no letters had been received for several months.

Although the soldiers carried their Vicksburg paroles, which should have protected them from molestation, they were unwilling to put them to the test, not being sufficiently trusting of Yankee largesse, and accordingly, avoided all Yankee military authorities along the way, and kept a circumspect eye, as though they had been fugitives from the law.

Eventually the little band of Confederates crossed the Sabine River. Along the way, they were dependent upon the country folk for shelter and sustenance. The travelers noticed a rather dejected feeling on the part of the people they encountered, although the citizenry cheerfully refused to accept any payment for food or lodging from the returning soldiers.

When the party at last entered Jackson County, they proceeded toward Texana. Their spirits were lifted as they once more trod upon land which they feared they would never see again. The country folks they had made contact with, cautioned them that the Federals had made good their boast to return with a body of troops, although the actual number was small, and hardly counted an army, and numbered only the size of a regiment.

"The Yanks are here, somewhere," said Major Simons, "the Home Guard can only watch from afar. We must keep a sharp lookout and to be on our guard."

"I am so happy to be home, to care much about a small reconnaissance-in-force," said Stayton.

All at once the merry band of comrades came upon a scene of great waste, a desolate-looking field, containing a clump of towering Live Oak trees, and a mansion which the Yankees had burnt to the ground. There were no fences marking the fields, and it appeared that an effort had been made to obliterate any landmarks.

"I feel that I recognize something familiar," said Major Simons, "those peach trees by the garden fence! The lawn, the olive trees, the gardens, the stables, the ancient Cedar trees, — this is the mansion of Captain Victor LaBauve!"

"Yes, or rather the ghost of it," said William Stayton, "What a state of desolation! Many a good time have I had in the good old mansion, laughed a good mite during our parties and barbecues. Now it's a pile of burnt bricks and two chimneys," then he said, almost to himself: "Why it was burned?"

"To show what happens to the home of a 'rebel.' To show there is no going back," said Major Simons.

"Barbarity is what I say. It is jes wan-ton barbarity," said Stayton.

Many articles of value were scattered about — among which was part of a sterling silver tea service, and many ancient tomes from a fine library. The books that had not been burnt, had been ruined having been tossed in the muddy fields, thrown about, the pages ripped out, and rained upon until they were saturated with moisture.

It was the past and present that occupied the minds of the little band of sojourners — the recollection of the bright scenes of other years, set suddenly against this dark picture of ruin. From the shattered Oaks and trodden flowers, the genius of the place seemed to look out, somber and hopeless.

Such was the scene at the LaBauve plantation on that August day in 1863. The enemy had laid waste along their route, and the countryside was marked by the burned houses where they had applied the torch. It was useless and barbarous to burn these private dwelling-houses; the wanton indulgence of spite and hatred on the part of the Yankees, who destroy in order to destroy.

Chapter Twenty-Seven

Many waters gladly meet in the Bays that glimmer nigh you,
And with names of beauty greet, gliding down to Pass Cavallo,
Bubbling now in music sweet, rolling thro' the Pass Cavallo,
Lost where the madden'd breakers meet, down beyond the Pass Cavallo.
— *The Soldier's Song of Pass Cavallo*

Lucy Bertram had at last reached "Seven Up," the Wiseman ranch on the banks of the West Carancahua. The Yankees had not damaged this part of the county, and "Seven Up" had remained intact. Miss Bertram gave the lock of hair, the memorandum book, the watch, and Wright Wiseman's other earthly possessions, to his mother. One of these items was a tintype of a young lady. Presumably, this was the same girl he had written the verses to, although none of the family could recognize her, and Miss Bertram never learned her identity.

His mother, Sarah Wiseman, was a widow who was attempting to keep the ranch viable despite the absence of her sons in the Confederate army in Mississippi and Tennessee, and the effects of the blockade and embargo. She was grateful for the return of the personal items, although it seemed the personal loss had quite naturally dampened the old lady's enthusiasm for the war. The only consolation was that all the neighboring families had suffered similar experiences of the loss of young sons, husbands, brothers and grandsons.

There being no "Home Guard" able to mount any resistance, the Yankee expeditionary force had free rein in Jackson County. A sort of un-official martial law had been imposed by the Federal authorities, the exercise thereof the local civilian authorities never questioned, as they had no power to enforce any kind of authority or any resistance to the Yankees.

Colonel Hagenbach, the same brutal Yankee that had probed up the Lavaca, Navidad, and Carancahua rivers earlier in the year, was in command once again.

He was welcomed by Brackenridge.

"I hope you have brought a larger number of soldiers this time, Colonel," said Brackenridge.

"About the same number as last, but I can move more swiftly with a smaller force. Rest assured we have plenty of ammunition and supplies in our wagons. When the war is concluded, which cannot be too far away, we will divide this countryside into military districts. We will need some loyal men to fill some posts, as military governors. I can count on you, Brackenridge, I hope?"

"Of course, Colonel."

"I am establishing my headquarters at the Ruins located outside town, near the Rebel Clark Owen's plantation, Rokeby," Hagenbach said.

The smile on Brackenridge's face disappeared when Hagenbach said this.

"I advise against that location, Colonel!" exclaimed Brackenridge.

"Why the devil not?" said Hagenbach.

The smile returned to Brackenridge's face. "Well," he said as he recovered his composure, "of course I do not believe a word of it, but the locals regard that place as benighted, a place where … people have been known to … never return from. I cannot express it in any other way," said Brackenridge.

"Enough of that childish nonsense, Brackenridge," said Hagenbach.

"Also", added Brackenridge, "there has been a near panic lately over the Wild Man of the Navidad. Citizens have reported numerous incidents where articles have been taken at night. Organized patrols at night have been unsuccessful in locating the culprit, although it was believed that the dogs had him treed last night, down along the West Carancahua, but somehow he eluded them," said Brackenridge.

Colonel Hagenbach merely ignored all of Brackenridge's concerns, as he shuffled some papers, and said in a curt, military manner:

"I do not have any authority to enter into matters concerning the superstitions of the ignorant citizenry. I must be going, Brackenridge. I have no reports of any local militia operating in the area. Therefore, I have no plans to fortify or entrench my camp. Feel free to call upon me at my new headquarters at the Ruins," said Colonel Hagenbach.

"Undoubtedly we will see each other. You are addressing the current owner of Rokeby, Colonel," said Brackenridge.

"Well, well," smiled Hagenbach, "how did that occur?"

"Yes, an unfortunate event," said Brackenridge making a sad expression, "Mrs. Owen, fine Southern lady that she is, but certainly no head for business, suddenly found herself at the mercy of her creditors. It seems the good Clark Owen overextended himself with his business dealings, he had mortgaged the property to the hilt. … I was able to come up with the financing, and with the agreement of the creditors, acquire the plantation, and helped her out."

"Helped her right out of a plantation," said Hagenbach, "Yes, I imagine you had plenty of gold on hand from your Charles Stillman activities."

"Fortune has smiled upon all my labors, Colonel" said Brackenridge, "well good day to you Colonel."

Colonel Hagenbach and his escort resumed their trek to the Ruins. Brackenridge returned to Rokeby, where he had an appointment with a landscape architect from the East.

It just so happened that on that day, Richard Austin Howard was visiting incognito the old plantation that he had so frequently visited before the war, and the little brick building that had contained the precious books that Colonel Owen was kind enough to loan him.

Brackenridge saw Howard walking up the gravel drive toward where he stood talking to the landscape architect. As he got closer and closer, he could hardly believe his eyes, and he could have sworn that he had seen a ghost, and that Old Colonel Clark Owen was returned to the earth. Brackenridge had never known Howard, or, as the reader can probably divine, we should now identify him as: the young Master Owen grown to manhood.

"What can I do for you, sir?" asked Brackenridge.

"I am looking for any of the family that reside here," answered Howard.

"You are speaking to the owner, sir," said Brackenridge, "I am George Brackenridge, owner of Rokeby."

"I see. I am Richard Howard. I used to be a guest here occasionally of the Owen family. Do you mind if I visit a place I knew when I was younger?" said Howard.

Brackenridge vaguely recalled that a person by the name of Howard was suspected of having destroyed quite a bit of Federal property in Texas and other parts of the South, as well as being responsible for shipping beef to the army in Virginia and thought immediately about placing him under arrest. Prior to that, however, it might behoove Brackenridge to see just how much Howard, or Owen, knew about his own background.

Howard walked up to the elaborate motto engraved in stone in the archway over the gravel path leading up to the manor house.

"Our Right Makes Our Might," he read out loud, "that is a fine motto. I have often thought how that motto was particularly suited for Colonel Owen. He was one of the most principled men I ever knew."

"Yes, I suppose so, however, my family, the Brackenridge's have a motto that may be taking its place on the stone archway. Our motto is "To the Strong goes the Prize."

" I think the former the better of the two," said Howard.

" Perhaps, but in any event, I have great plans for Rokeby. The first order of business is to pull down that old portion of the edifice that Colonel Owen let stand. The rock will make good fill material for some low-lying areas on the grounds," said Brackenridge.

" It seems such a shame to pull down that venerable pile! It is part of the antiquity of Texas," said Howard.

" In its place will go a new modern addition, " said Brackenridge.

" A pity," Howard reiterated.

" Nevertheless, sometimes things must give way to a new order. I also wish to build a lumber planning mill on that eminence that overlooks those old Ruins."

" But that would mean cutting down that mighty Oak! That tree that has sheltered the white man and red man for eight hundred years? Surely you would not topple such a tree as that!" said Howard.

" As you can plainly see, the lightning bolt has practically severed the Oak in two, it needs to come down."

Brackenridge resented Howard's impertinence: "How came you to this place?" asked Brackenridge.

" I have lately been away in Houston on personal business," answered Howard, wanting to be vague.

"A strong young man like yourself I would have thought would be in the army during times like these," asked Brackenridge.

"And I would answer you back with the same query about yourself," said Howard, as he continued to look around the grounds to see what changes had occurred since he had gone off to the war.

"I am the local agent for the United States Treasury Department, authorized to issue permits for trade, to take possession of and manage abandoned plantations and other property," said Brackenridge.

Howard's train of thought, however, had returned to the entablature with the carved motto over the archway, and he said, almost to himself:

"It is odd, that motto of the Owen's. I had a very sad childhood. My earliest memories, however, are of a happy place, before I was separated from my mother and father. Where this place was, I know not. But I remember being rocked by my Mammy, as I sat watching beneath a massive tree draped in Ivy vines. Not unlike that very tree you speak of. There was a great valley spread out in front of us, that this location looked out upon. She sang me a song that had a similar line:

'The dark shall be light, And the wrong made right, When … I believe it was … Owen's right and Owen's might Shall meet on' — I cannot remember the last line — on some particular height; HEIGHT is the rhyme, I am sure; but I cannot hit upon the preceding word."

Brackenridge's face went pale, and he said nothing.

"And I seem to remember," continued Howard/Owen, "a little story my Mammy used to tell me about a mighty Oak tree, who was bound up by an Ivy vine, after being riven in two, just like the one on the eminence above the Ruins."

"You remember far too much," thought Brackenridge to himself, "far too much for my comfort. You are about to recall that your first years were on Rokeby Heights." Therefore, Brackenridge thought of a plan to extricate himself from this perilous situation.

" You say your name is Howard?"

" Yes."

" It seems I recall something about that name. I believe Colonel Hagenbach mentioned he was looking for a man named Howard," said Brackenridge.

" I believe it is some other Howard he is seeking. I have never left Texas. The man he is looking for is in the Confederate service," said Howard.

"He was suspected of various acts of sabotage and worse, in and out of Texas, for that matter. And I believe I have the right man, and that you are that man. I am placing you in custody, until Colonel Hagenbach can take charge of you. Do you resist?"

" No, but I hope that when you realize you have the wrong man, you are justly punished for your mistake."

Brackenridge made a gesture with his hands to two blue-clad soldiers, watching from a distance, whereupon they made a beeline to either side of Howard, and he was instructed to accompany them to where the Federal Colonel Hagenbach was setting up his headquarters, at the nearby Ruins.

Chapter Twenty-Eight

> Oh! yes, I am a Southern girl, and glory in the name,
> And boast it with far greater pride than glittering wealth or fame.
> We envy not the Northern girl, her robes of beauties rare,
> Though diamonds grace her snowy neck, and pearls bedeck her hair.
> — *The Homespun Dress*

Lucy Bertram stayed on at Seven Up at the request of Wright's mother: "We cannot afford to show you much society, what with the war and everything rationed and shortages, but we can show you some pretty summer days and maybe something of the life we experienced before the war. Not all the romance has gone from the scene," said the matriarch, Sarah Wiseman.

"Lizzie (Wright's younger sister) can show you how we pass the time here at Seven Up," added Sarah, "Maybe even take up a barn dance or quilting bee. We do not have much occasion to entertain these days, but we would be mighty glad to try and show our appreciation to you for all you did for Wright."

"The war has spoiled everything! No one is having any parties or anything!" complained sixteen-year-old Lizzie Wiseman.

"Now hush Lizzie! No moping around, daughter! Most every family has suffered some personal loss. It would be easier to bear if it were not for the meanness and gloating of the Yankees around here. Why the other day, one of our neighbors was planning a funeral for a loved one, and they had to apply to the Federal authorities for a permit. Imagine that!" said Sarah, with a pained expression on her face.

Lucy Bertram, never one to shy away when there was work to be done, was welcomed into the Carancahua community. The household of Sarah Wiseman now was made up of herself, her daughter Lizzie, son William, (now returned from his war service), and her two younger boys, James and Albert, along with a faithful old Negro foreman, and his wife. Sarah had managed to keep the Seven Up profitable, despite all the disruptions of the war years.

The Wiseman household, like every other household along the two Carancahuas, sought to give support and assistance to the men and boys fighting the war. Material was transformed and converted to fill a present need. Carpets were made into blankets, and young ladies' dresses were made into shirts for the soldiers. Linen was made into lint for their wounds.

The survival of the plucky young nation was remarkable since money was almost as unavailable as material. Confederate bonds and money were yet in their infancy. All resources were cut off. The survival of the new nation was dependent on the armies, but the Government could not provide sufficient food and clothing and ammunition for its armies. Thus arose a situation that put women's wit to the test. Spinning-wheels, looms and dye-pots were soon brought into requisition. Wool of home production was especially converted, by loving hands, into warm flannels and heavy garments, with soft scarfs and snugly filled leggings, to shield the Texas boys from the Northern clime.

Societies were formed to provide supplies for the general demand of the army. Texan homes withheld nothing that could add to the soldier's comfort. Every available fragment of material was converted into a garment. Old men and little boys were occupied in winding thread and holding brooches, and even knitting on the socks when the mystery of "turning the heel" had been passed. The little spinning-wheel, turned by a treadle, became a fascination to the girls, and with its busy hum was mingled often, the merry strain of patriotic songs:

Our wagon's plenty big enough, the running gear is good,
'Tis stuffed with cotton round the sides and made of Southern wood.
Carolina is the driver, with Georgia by her side —
Virginia 'll hold our Flag up and we'll all take a ride.
Wait for the wagon,
The Dissolution wagon,
The South is our wagon
And we'll all take a ride!

Even those women who had been reared in ease and affluence soon learned practically that "necessity is the mother of invention," and the story of their ingenuity might surprise their Northern sisters who regarded them as soft, pleasure loving members of society. The war certainly brought out the true woman, and no woman of any age or nation ever entered, heart and soul, more enthusiastically into their country's contest than those who supported the "Lost Cause."

However, sometimes it was hard for sixteen-year-old girls to endure.

"I wish the war would end so that we can start having parties!" exclaimed Lizzie.

"No more carrying on about parties, now, child, I promised Old Mr.

Burnett to try and help him free Davey," said Sarah.

"Why, what's happened to Davey?" asked Lucy Bertram.

"Have you not heard? He has been arrested on an accusation of being a spy," said Lizzie.

"How could that happen?" asked Lucy.

"Well, you know how Davey loves hearing his songs and sticks his pockets full of his scraps of papers with songs and lyrics. He is a paroled soldier, is subject to search at any time by the Provost Marshal's office. And he was searched, and was found to possess coded messages," said Sarah.

"Everyone knows those scraps of paper he stuffs in his pockets are filled with the incoherent words and phrases he jots down. He practically has a language all his own, something partly English and partly made up in his own head," she added.

"Yes, you know, and I know but it seems the Yankees do not know this. He is suspected with having sent secret communications to the Confederates."

"This is ridiculous!" exclaimed Lucy, "I must make my way to Major Howard."

"Major Howard done been arrested too," said the servant Ben, "and he done been taken to de Ruins whar de Yankees have set up a Head-Quatahs in de tunnels dere. And ah seen Miss Kate Dandridge, sure as de world, jes ridin' along wid dem big Yankees dat went thru town."

"Are you sure it was Kate, why would she have reason to come back here at this time?' asked Sarah.

"It was her jes the same, and ah took mah hat off and said: 'Its nice ter see you again, Miss Kate,' and you know she neber said a word t' me? When she done looked at me, she turned her head away," said Ben dejectedly.

"She's not the same person as the one you knew, Ben," said Lizzie, "nor the same person whom Wright ..." and she could not finish her sentence.

"Howze dat, Miss Lizzie, did de Yankees conjure some spell on her?" asked Ben.

"No, the Yankees did not, but ... I do think, Ben ... that your notion of conjuring puts me in mind of a person who may help us! I think we need to speak with old Flora, and see what light she can shed on things," said Lucy Bertram.

"You had best be careful, child, if you do attempt to see Flora. The colored folk are all riled up. It seems that there have been recent accounts of houses entered at night and the only things taken were a loaf of bread sitting out. And some rusty tools lying about were taken, only to be returned a few days later, just as mysteriously, during the night, polished to perfection by an unknown process," said Sarah.

"Yes, and valuable jewelry in plain sight is not touched," added Lizzie.

"Just the thing we needed with everything else going on, for the Wild Man to be stirring things up," said Sarah, and turned to Ben: "Ben you drive Miss Lucy and keep a sharp lookout. Take your pistol with you. If any danger arises, you get her out of there."

"Yes'm, but how do we find Miss Florah? Do we have to go to de Witches' Grot? Ah've dun ben tol nevuh tuh go dere," said Ben.

"The only thing I know to do is to ask some of the colored ladies at Rokeby, they should know where to find her," said Sarah.

"I want William to go with you, also," said Sarah upon considering the matter.

"Mother," said Lizzie, "if he is well enough. You know since he came home from Vicksburg, he hasn't been the same. He is still weak, and I would …"

"Would what?" said William, in a loud voice, as he hurriedly entered the room where the conversation had been taking place, "Ah am fully recovered from my sickness," he added, knowing full well that he was not recovered.

"If William wants to go, then do so," was Sarah's final pronouncement. "I will take you to the ladies that can lead you to Flora," said William.

It was then that William, Lucy and Ben climbed into the buggy pulled by a pair of dapple-gray horses. The buggy then traveled down the long driveway that led from the Seven Up Ranch, and a half hour later reached the little row of cabins inhabited by the Negro servants of Rokeby.

The women were seated in a circle outside attending to various chores, and when they saw the buggy approach, looked up with a concerned look upon their faces. As soon as they recognized Ben and William, their careworn features relaxed.

"Well if it ain't Ben and Marse Will'um home from de wah! An who dis?" said one of the ladies, who was known as Emmaline.

"Dis here is Miss Lucy Bertram. She is de lady from de Blue Grass dat nursed Marse Wright at Vicksburg," said Ben.

"Wha' can we do for you folks?" they asked.

"We are looking for Miss Flora, if you please, do you know where we can find her?" said William pointedly.

"Yes, we know, but why?" was the response.

"The Yankees have set up their headquarters in the underground labyrinth at the Ruins, and we believe that Flora may know about them. One of the soldiers back from the war, Davey Burnett, was taken there by the Yankees and kept," said Lucy, "also Major Howard."

"Do you believe in conjure?" asked one of the Negresses.

"Conjure?" asked William.

"Ah can see by yo faces you doubt," said Emmaline with a smile.

"I suppose we are taught to believe our senses, rather than fanciful stories," said William.

"Then you will not find Flora to be of any help, child. For ah assure you, Flora does believe in it. De unseen world. We have all seen things that teach us der is another world," said Emmaline.

"And we all know that signs, sperits, an conjure is real," she added.

"Yes," chimed in one of the other women seated, " if you are eating with a mouthful of food and sneeze, that sho is a true sign of death. I know 'cause years ago I wuz havin' breakfast wit my son Wylie and Wylie sneezed and said, 'Mama I'm so sorry I jist couldn't help it the sneeze came on me so quick,' Two weeks later my mother died. That is one sign that's true, yes sir."

"If a picture falls off the wall someone in the family will die," said another.

"If you dream about teeth, if one falls out dats another sign of death," added one of the ladies.

They all expressed to the visitors their own ideas and experiences.

"Jest as sho as your left-hand itches you will receive money."

"If the left side of your nose itches a man is coming to the house. If it itches on the top, he will come ridin'."

"If the right side of your nose itches a woman is comin' to de house."

"Yes, yes, yes, I am sure you believe this is all true, but what does it have to do with Flora and the Yankees at the Ruins?" asked William.

"Hush, now be still," said an aged Negro woman who had white hair and appeared to be the oldest and wisest of the group, "ah will tell you why: on the old road that goes past de Ruins dere is a cemetery that is next to the road, and in dis cemetery is a stone building, a receiving vault, is what dey call it, an dis building has a door in de floor dat leads down to de tunnels connected to de Ruins. But dis cemetery is hanted, dey say dat an old woman dat wuz one hunn'red years old was a witch, an wuz buried dere. Now dis witch wuz so awful, dat dis spot is hanted. Ah have known horses to run away right dere wit people and hurt dem. Den sometimes dey have rared and kicked and turned to go in de other direction. You

or The Maid of Saragoza

see, horses can see things sometimes where folks can't."

Then the aged woman came directly to the point: "Flora can be found at her cave at de Witches' Grot. Do you know where dat is?

" I believe I do, although I have never actually been there," said William.

" Dat old Sea Cap'n knows where dat witches' cave is," said one of the women, "ask him t' sho you."

"Talk to her an see if she can help you. I don't know if'un she will. But ah shore nuff would try if ah wuz you," said Emmaline.

"An if'un you do need ter git down in dem tunnels, you can enter dem at dat hanted cemetery. But once you enter dem tunnels, you will be at de mercy of dem dat believes in conjure."

"Thank you, ladies" said William as he smiled, doffed his cap, and left with the others of his party, to find the Old Sea Captain, John Billups.

Chapter Twenty-Nine

Season of mists and mellow fruitfulness,
    Close bosom-friend of the maturing sun,
Conspiring with him how to load and bless
    With fruit the vines that round the thatch-eves run,
To bend with apples the moss'd cottage-trees,
    And fill all fruit with ripeness to the core.
To swell the gourd, and plump the hazel shells
    With a sweet kernel, to set budding more,
And still more, later flowers for the bees,
    Until they think warm days will never cease,
For Summer has o'er-brimm'd their clammy cells.

— *To Autumn*

A November mist overspread the prairies and pastures, as the Sea Captain, John Billups, slowly but steadily rode his horse on the road which ran between Texana and his home along the West Carancahua. He was struck with a feeling of melancholy inspired by the scene and by the season.

The West Carancahua, still only a trickling rivulet, seemed to murmur as if oppressed with the departure of autumn. Among the scattered copses which here and there fringed its banks, the oak-trees only retained that pallid green that precedes their russet hue. The leaves of other trees were most of them stripped from the branches, and lay rustling at each breath of wind, and disturbed by every step of the horse.

The old gentlemen dropped into the natural train of thought which these autumnal emblems of mortal hopes are peculiarly calculated to inspire.

"There," he said to himself, looking at the leaves which lay strewed around, "lie the hopes of early youth, first formed that they may soonest wither, and loveliest in Spring to become most contemptible in Winter. But you lingerers," he added, looking to a copse of beeches which still bore their withered leaves, "you are the proud plans of adventurous manhood, formed later, and still clinging to the mind of age, although it acknowledges their inanity! None lasts save the foliage of the mighty Oak, which only begins to show itself when the rest of the forest has enjoyed half its existence. A pale and decayed hue is all it possesses, but still, it retains that symptom of vitality to the last. So let it be with Captain John

Billups! My hopes are trodden under foot like yon neglected withered leaves — to the dreams of manhood I look back as to fancy illusions, of which the pith and existence has long since faded; but my Faith and my determination to serve God, shall remain supporting me through these tempestuous times!"

While moving along in this contemplative mood, he became aware of the approach of the buggy bearing the party of young people, attempting to secure the freedom of their friends.

"Hello there, Captain Billups!" shouted William.

"Why hello there, children, why do ye hasten so?"

William hurriedly explained the nature of their quest.

"Yes," said the Captain, "I have been to the Witches' Grot and can lead you there."

Meanwhile, miles away, in the underground labyrinth beneath the Ruins, in which the Yankee Colonel Hagenbach had established his headquarters and his prison cells for Richard Austin Howard and Davey Burnett, an interrogation was taking place.

Richard Austin Howard, alone, was taken from his makeshift cell in the tunnels, and led to the office of Hagenbach, which had been hastily constructed with heavy wooden partitions and iron bars.

Hagenbach was seated on a chair behind a small table on which documents and various papers were scattered, when Howard was led into the presence of Hagenbach.

"Ah, Major Howard, how kind of you to come, please have a seat," said Hagenbach sarcastically, "I hope your accommodations meet with your approval."

Howard neither smiled nor showed any emotion.

"I take it I have stated your correct rank?"

"There must be a different Howard you are mistaking me for. I have never been in the Confederate army, " replied Howard.

"Come now, Major, let's not insult each other with childish games. …"

"I am sorry, but I am not the man you are looking for."

"Major, a quite impressive file you have. Let's see here … (Hagenbach started to read through a file he had on the desk). "Attended West Point but did not graduate. Worked as a land surveyor. Made important friends and were an aide to General Bee at … 'Bull Run' … or do you Southerners prefer 'Manassas'? Desperately wounded carrying messages during that battle. Assigned to the Trans-Mississippi Department Commissary Subsistence, captured on the Red River running cattle across the Mississippi. Detained due to documents indicating your importance to the Confederacy."

"Yes, this man's record seems an impressive one." answered Howard.

"Come now, let's not play games! You are this man" shouted Hagenbach.

After Hagenbach had resumed his composure, his demeanor changed to even more seriousness.

You forget that we have spies operating amongst your people too! Oh yes, quite! We know exactly who you are and what you are. The Order of the Red Camellia, oh yes, we know about your attempts with the Yellow Fever. The doctor in Kentucky, you worked with him to send clothing north infected with the Yellow Fever did you not! That is a serious offense, Major, very serious!"

"You have the wrong man," was all that Howard would say.

"You have just about exhausted my patience, Major. Here is the offer of my government. You sign a confession detailing your actions on behalf of the Confederate Government, that clarify that everything you did was ordered by the President at Richmond, and I have been authorized by President Lincoln to offer you a full and complete and absolute pardon for any acts you may have or have committed from the beginning of time, to today, and you will be allowed to go home, and will be unmolested, so long as you do not take up any further arms against the North. Here is the confession, read it," said Hagenbach as he placed some documents in front of Howard.

Howard read the documents Hagenbach had given him.

"These papers implicate the President and his ministers in the Yellow Fever scheme?" asked Howard.

"Yes, and they correctly recite the facts, do they not? And all you have to do is sign them. You will be given a full and complete pardon."

Howard made a frown as he looked up from the papers, pushed them towards Hagenbach, and said: "I will not sign them."

"Then suffer the consequences!" said Hagenbach, as he snatched back the documents, and Howard was returned to his little damp cell in the labyrinth beneath the Ruins.

Chapter Thirty

Sound, sound the clarion, fill the fife!
To all the sensual world proclaim,
One crowded hour of glorious life
Is worth an age without a name.

— *Old Mortality,* Chapter 34

The Old Sea Captain was somewhat skeptical about the likelihood that Flora would give any assistance in freeing the two captives and took issue with the Negro ladies at Rokeby concerning the powers of conjuring, but nevertheless, he agreed to show the young people the location of the Witches' Grot.

The party descended the little slope down to the side of the creek, and the intrepid party entered the entrance to the cave. The furnishings and fixtures looked about the same as the last time Billups had been in the cave, the last year before the war. No one appeared to be present, although a fire was burning low in the pit.

"She is not here. She was our Anchor to Windward, and I am afraid we will not be able to do any good," said the Old Sea Captain.

" I think I might know where she can be found," said William, "it was a place she frequented, and we young boys growing up, before we were old enough to understand, used to make fun of her for singing her wild songs and her imaginary friends. Later we understood better that she was mortified by the fact that one of the little children she was taking care of, one of her charges, disappeared and she was blamed for it."

"It was Colonel Owen's boy, from what I have been told," said Lucy.

"Yes," said William.

"If she is at the place where I think she is, it is not too far away," said William, "it is a gigantic Oak tree that has been riven practically in two, by a lightning strike, and is covered in an English Ivy vine," he added, "on a knoll overlooking the ruins."

The party then proceeded along the road leading to the Oak tree overlooking the Ruins.

The Captain, along the way, continued his pensive train of thought that the time of year had inspired: "I still remember when I heard that Wright and Zack Oppenheimer had been killed at Vicksburg. Wright showed such promise as an artist and had rare talents. And as a Poet, he had only begun to sing his Muse. I am quite certain that, had he lived, he

or The Maid of Saragoza

would have left some poem or work of art, to make himself remembered. And Zack was such a hard worker at his shop."

"Wright died a hero's death, something I may not get an opportunity to do," said William.

"When I think of death, William, as a thing worth thinking of, it is in the hope of pressing one day some well-fought and hard-won field of battle and dying with the shout of victory in my ear — that would be worth dying for, and more, it would be worth having lived for!" said Captain Billups.

"Some say," said Lucy, "that Wright's spirit was sunk so low about Miss Dandridge, that he was despondent and became misanthropic."

"I do not know that to be true," said the Old Sea Captain, "from what I observed. He accompanied myself on many a foray into the countryside, while I was on my searches for LaSalle's fort. He would sketch the scenery while I dug trenches and walked the fields after each hard rain. Wright seemed to be happy. He believed he had been cruelly jilted, it is true, but is it not true that scarce one out of twenty of young persons will marry their first love, and scarce one out of twenty of the remainder has cause to rejoice at having done so. I think his conception of Miss Dandridge was more of a fanciful creation he had made up in his mind, than an actual reality."

The party arrived near the location of the knoll, and Flora could be seen in the distance, seated beneath the towering riven Oak, just as had been predicted.

"Here we have arrived," said the Sea Captain in a low voice, "let us keep quiet, so as not to startle her. I will climb up the path that leads to the summit. I will go alone, you wait here. If we approach in a group that might startle her."

As the Sea Captain drew nearer, he could see that Flora had what appeared to be a corn-husk baby, wrapped in a blanket, and was rocking to and fro.

"Poor deluded soul," thought the Captain, "she has completely lost her wits."

He observed that Flora appeared to be singing a song of some kind, and he could only make out some of the words:
The Brown Man of the Moor that stays
  Beneath the heather bell ... was all he could make out.

This was a reference to the Wild Man of the Navidad, thought the Captain, and this confirmed the Captain's prior suspicions, that somehow, these two personages, Flora and the Wild Man, were connected.

Flora made some gesticulations with her hands, as she continued to rock the corn-husk baby.

He at length decided the moment was right to attempt to engage her in conversation: "Miss Flora, Miss Flora, halloo! I have come to have a palaver with ye."

"Approach, Captain John Billups," said the woman whose wild-eyes and maniacal ramblings seemed to justify those who called her a witch.

"I come to …"

However just as the Sea Captain was preparing to explain his mission, he was interrupted by the Witch.

"I know why you have come. Approach and see my charge, young Master Owen."

"That is a corn husk baby like the girls play with," said Billups, wanting to direct her mind to the present.

"No, this is my charge, young Master Owen."

"No, young Master Owen is dead, Flora," said Billups.

"Oh, is he?" said Flora with a slight smile on her face.

The Captain changed the topic of the discussion: "Flora, who is the Brown Man of the Moor?"

"Do you not know? He that visits folk's homes, but takes not valuables, only food."

"Yes, and he is also called the Wild Man of the Navidad? Is he not?" said the Captain. "Flora, do you know him or what he is? Is he man or ghost?"

"He is a mystery to me. He walks at midnight. Here is my charge," said Flora as she continued to rock the corn husk baby.

Captain Billups was becoming increasingly concerned for Flora's mental sanity.

She continued to ramble on: "You see the mighty Oak riven by the lightning?" (Flora motioned to the gigantic Live Oak overhead, that had been struck by a bolt from the sky and nearly cleft in two.) "It tells of the sufferings of the young men killed in the war, and the old men who will be killed in the peace. It tells of the burned houses by the Twin Vandals, Grant and Sherman. It tells of how the war made enemies of the men who had held our plow handles and stood around our tables. The young men can hope, but to the old men, their lands will be made valueless or confiscated. …

She continued: "Now then, do you see that vine binding up the shattered tree and hiding its wounds? That is the Southern woman clinging closer and more tenderly to father and husband when the storms beat upon them, comforting as only such Christian women can comfort, helping only as such heroines can help. …"

Captain Billups came to realize that his concerns about Flora's sanity were groundless.

"Yes Flora, you have always been a wise counsel. As bad as the war has been, I too fear the conquest by the North will be even worse for the Southern people," said the Old Sea Captain.

Flora was able to point out to the Captain that the entrance to the subterranean tunnels, at the Ruins, was heavily posted with guards who would contest any attempt to enter the tunnels and rescue the two prisoners.

"I will lead you to an old cemetery not far from here, where we can enter," said Flora.

Just as had been predicted, the receiving vault in the "haunted" cemetery had a heavy wooden door in the floor, covered up by a carpet. Our friends climbed down the ladder to the tunnel system below the ground. Having brought lamps, and there being no Yankees or other persons near to impede their movement, the intrepid little party was able to light their way along the tunnel that Flora said would lead to where their friends were being held.

Flora seemed to know the direction to go, as the main tunnel was occasionally intersected by other tunnels, yet she never wavered from the path she was treading. The tunnels appeared to have been built many years ago, by an unknown people: the stones used to construct it having been carved and moulded in a fashion that would have been unknown to the native Indian tribes.

The party eventually neared an area quite obviously used by the Yankees, as it was possible to detect the loud voices of the Yankee troops echoing down the corridor, engaging each other with shouts and laughter.

Ben, with his eyes wide with apprehension, whispered to the Sea Captain: "Cap'n, jes what is de plan, once we find de Yankees?"

The Captain turned and smiled: "Well, Ben, don't cha know, son? We are gonna use conjure on the Yankees."

"Dats good cause all we got in firearms is dis here pistol of mine. An ah ain't nebber fired dis here gun off once. Ah don't eben know how it works!"

"Now is a fine time to tell us, Ben. Maybe one of you other soldiers have a plan?"

Flora said the two captives were in some passages a good distance away from the part occupied by the loud Yankee soldiers, and the group followed her down another of the seemingly endless system of tunnels.

"We have to find out where Howard and Davey are being held. Down one of these dark passages, I reckon, " said William.

Captain Billups suddenly had an idea, and he said to William Wiseman: "Can you sing *Maryland My Maryland*?"

"Yes, but why?"

"Just sing the first verse, son, as loud as you can. I have a notion it will get a pretty quick reaction."

William sang out in a clear voice: "The despot's heel is on thy shore, Maryland! My Maryland! His torch is at thy temple door, Maryland! My Maryland!"

"That's it, boy, sing it!" said Billups.

"Avenge the patriotic gore, That flecked the streets of Baltimore, And be the battle queen of yore, Maryland! My Maryland!"

The Captain cocked his head slightly as if trying to hear any response. No sounds were heard.

"Try another verse," he said.

Again, William sang out:

> Dear Mother! burst the tyrant's chain,
> Maryland! My Maryland!
> Virginia should not call in vain,
> Maryland! My Maryland!
> She meets her sisters on the plain —
> "Sic semper!" 'tis the proud refrain
> That baffles minions back amain,
> Maryland! My Maryland!

This time there was a frantic clanging noise coming from one of the dark passages. Flora hurriedly strode down toward the clanging noise.

Captain Billups was laughing and singing the last verse as he walked: "Old Maryland! Tis' where I was born, boys, 'I hear the distant thunder-hum, Maryland! The Old Line's bugle, fife and drum … (he laughed as he sung)… Maryland … She is not dead, nor deaf, nor dumb — Huzza, she spurns the Northern scum! She …"

Suddenly the party came to the source of the noise and shown their lamp upon the diminutive form of Davy Burnett, unable to speak, but well able to clang the metal cup which he had been provided, on the make-shift jail cell that had been constructed by the Yankees. Major Richard Austin Howard, however, was nowhere to be seen.

or The Maid of Saragoza

Chapter Thirty-One

> But Enoch yearn'd to see her face again,
> If I might look on her sweet face again
> And know that she is happy.' So, the thought
> Haunted and harass'd him, and drove him forth,
> At evening when the dull November day
> Was growing duller twilight, to the hill.
> There he sat down gazing on all below,
> There did a thousand memories roll upon him,
> Unspeakable for sadness.
> — *Enoch Arden At The Window*

Major Howard had been led from his cell to the office of Colonel Hagenbach, but much to his surprise, the figure which was awaiting him was one of a feminine form. Yes, it had been many years since he had seen her, but he still recognized the person who he was to speak with, and as Ben had already identified in a previous chapter, Kate Forbes, the former Kate Dandridge, had indeed returned home.

"You are surprised to see me?"

"Quite," said Howard.

"Well, I thought I would see how you were, Richard. You were older than me, but I remember all of us children of various ages all went to school in Mrs. Chiver's house along the Carancahua. You always won the awards for reading the most books," said Kate.

" That is, until you were old enough to come to our school, and after that, you won all the awards for books read," said Howard.

Kate laughed and said, "I guess you have me there."

As they conversed about the old times, a flood of memories came back to Howard. After that, the current situation was addressed:

"I have good news, you are to be released," she said.

"That's, that's good news," said Howard.

She went on to recount how her husband had prevailed on Howard's behalf, with the authorities in Washington, who wanted, of course, to deal much more harshly with Howard.

"You may not realize that with the record you have accumulated, you have been ordered to be detained indefinitely by no less a person than Secretary Stanton himself!" she told him.

"Yes, Richard," she continued, "particularly with the information learned from some of our spies, about your involvement with the Red Camellia, it was quite a trick, then, to have persuaded the Administration to agree to release you, but my husband did it. I am to personally tell you this."

"Please express my gratitude, Kate," he told her.

Then he added, looking down at the ragged dirty clothes he had on: "I wish I were more presentable; I have not been able to wash or change clothes for a month. I am ashamed to be seen like this."

"Just sign these papers, and you are released," she said as she thrust some official looking documents in front of him.

He looked at the papers, trying to discern their meaning, having difficulty with focusing his eyes after being so long confined in semi-darkness. The papers appeared to have been prepared by the War Department. The meaning at length became clear to him. He realized the gravity of their terms, as they carefully laid out a complete confession placing all responsibility for the driving of the diseased cattle into the Federal camps, upon the President and his Cabinet in Richmond.

"I cannot sign these papers," he said as he handed the papers back to Mrs. Forbes.

"Please Richard, do not become a martyr for these Hotspurs. Sign," said Mrs. Forbes.

"I now see clearly why you are here and why you are telling me these things," said Howard. "Go," and he turned away and faced the wall of the cave.

"What good does it do you to sit in a filthy cell, awaiting the hangman's noose? Do you understand, these men, my husband, mean to hold someone accountable? Hold you accountable. Let it be the ones in Richmond," pleaded Mrs. Forbes.

" And what are you doing, turning against your own people?" asked Howard.

" This is not about me, Richard. But whether you believe it or not, I still have a fondness in my heart for Jackson County. That is why I am here. We are just beginning our plan to reconstruct this county. …"

"Reconstruct? What is that?" asked Howard, who had never heard this word used in this context.

"That is the term used by my husband and the others in Washington. The South will …"

"The South will what?" interrupted Howard, "Bend to the yoke of the Northern tyranny? You will dictate to the South what it must believe and what cannot believe? How we should live, according to your standards? What will you do, emancipate the Negro by carrying him away North? To what? Has it occurred to your friends in the North that we Southerners know our Negroes the best? That it might be best to gradually free them? After they have received a trade, a vocation with which to make a living? Not by just throwing them out into the world?" said Howard, with an emotional voice.

"Are you quite finished lecturing me?" she said.

"No, we will never bend to the yoke you wish to place on us. We may be defeated by superior numbers of men and materiel, but we will never be conquered," said Howard.

"Then prepared to be destroyed as a culture," she said, picking up the papers she had spread before Howard.

"You have imprisoned and intend to hang Davey Burnett?," said Howard. "He is an innocent. Let him go. He knows nothing about any codes. He cannot even speak."

"He had scraps of coded communications in his possession," said Mrs. Forbes, "I am sorry if he is a friend of yours."

"He is everybody's friend. He never met anybody that he did not like and has never hurt anyone. Even when he was a soldier, he was the fellow who was running to get more ammunition, running to fill canteens, so the boys say... He is innocent. Are there penalties for innocence in this New World of yours?" asked Howard.

Mrs. Forbes sat silent and grave at Howard's last remark, then cried out "Guard!" as she arose from the table at which they sat and walked away.

The guards entered and led Howard back to his cell. A few minutes passed, and he heard some voices from the dark tunnel that did not sound like the usual guffawing and banter of the Federal guards. These voices sounded familiar. Before long, appeared our little intrepid band of heroes, the Sea Captain, Will Wiseman, Ben, Davey Burnett and Lucy Bertram, all being led by the Sibyl Flora, holding a lamp to light the way.

"You are a sight for sore eyes!" said Howard, "Quick, if you men can all yank on this iron door, you can wrench it off its hinges … hurry before the guard makes his rounds. …"

"You'll never get the opportunity!" shouted a voice from the direction of the part of the tunnels occupied by the Yankees. It was Colonel Hagenbach, accompanied with several armed soldiers in blue, and George Brackenridge.

"Well, well, well, well" said a smiling Hagenbach, "What an honor to have such an august assemblage as this! We have the well-known explorer of the seas, quite out of your element, sir! And several Rebel scum have deigned to join us tonight! And the fair Miss Bertram beginning her criminal career. Who are these two niggers?"

"Shut your mouth you d__n fool, or I will shut it for you!" said Howard.

Hagenbach ignored the remark and merely said to Brackenridge: "Yes we will need some more cells constructed, Brackenridge, see to it that your tradesmen get to work." Then, to the blue-clad soldiers, he said: "Take them and confine them until you hear from me."

The prisoners were led to makeshift cells in one of the tunnels, except that Davey Burnett was led away for further examination.

"You had better not harm a hair on that boy's head," said Howard. "and you treat her (pointing to Flora) as she deserves to be treated."

"I have had just about enough of your insolence," said Hagenbach, "but I will not have to put up with it for much longer. You have all saved me the trouble of rounding you up. Guard, put these persons in separate cells, then join me as we attend to the Burnett boy."

The Yankees left with Davey Burnett in their clutches, and the remaining parties could all communicate with each other, even though in separate cells.

Flora suddenly shouted out: "Master Owen! It is time for you to avenge the wrong done to your House!" She was looking directly at Howard.

"Flora," said Howard, "you know that I have always had a vague notion that we have known each other in the past. That could not be true, could it?"

"We have known each other in the past, when you were little, I took care of you, young Master Owen," said Flora.

"Why do you insist on calling me that? Why do you address me as that?" said Howard.

"Young Master Owen, your time has arrived to fulfill the destiny that was foretold long ago. You are now twenty-five years of age, and the second crisis age has arrived. The planets and stars are aligned, and the time has come for you to help shake off the yoke of the invader. Reclaim what is rightfully yours:

> The dark shall be light,
> And the wrong made right,
> When Owen's right and Owen's might

Shall meet on Rokeby Height!

"Arise, and walk out of the cell, nothing made by man can hold you. Avenge the absconding of your father's house! And the subjugation of your country!"

"What can you tell me about my destiny? Who was my father?" asked Howard.

Before an answer could be made the door to Howard's cell opened as if by magic, and he was able to then free the others from their cells. The group proceeded to hurriedly walk down the tunnel to a location where the sounds of a desperate struggle was taking place. Along the way, Howard was questioning Flora about his identity.

Flora answered: "Do you not have eyes? Can you not see the father in the son?" Then she continued: "You were kidnapped from your parents, Clark Owen and Laura Owen, your father and mother, at age five. This was arranged by old John Adams Brackenridge, who did this to allow his son George Brackenridge to garner the Plantation. He said it was more likely that he could obtain "Rokeby" if no male heir was present to operate the Plantation..." Flora calmly continued her narration: "You were placed at the Orphanage in Victoria. The Howards, a childless couple, found you there and adopted you. It was pure coincidence that you became friends with Owen family, and your parents being humble, the good Colonel Owen allowed you to borrow books from his library, and treated you with kindness, all the time believing his real son, who would have been your age, had drown, or been taken away, or otherwise lost," she explained.

"Captain Clark Owen was my father?" asked Howard.

"Yes," answered Flora.

"How long have you known this?" asked Howard.

"Whether I knew it, when I knew it, are not important. Fate must be allowed to play itself out, Fate is stronger than we poor humans are — These things are what must inevitably occur on this Earth. They — the Fates — do not allow for personal feelings to be consulted," she said.

Captain Billups thought to himself: "If I ever had a doubt as to Flora's sanity, this has been removed. This woman not only has her wits, but she is also in contact with the unseen world, that the ladies at Rokeby were talking about."

Suddenly they entered a lighted room where a scaffolding had been erected, to see the lifeless body of Davey Burnett hanging from a rope by the neck, surrounded by the blue-clad soldiers. Hagenbach and Brackenridge were also there, smiling at the look of horror on the faces of the Captain, Howard, Lucy Bertram, Ben, and William Wiseman. Everyone seemed to be distressed but Flora, who alone seemed to be in control of her emotions.

The Sea Captain, seething with hatred and a desire for revenge, said to Brackenridge: "Flora has already disclosed to us what you and your father did to this poor boy (pointing at Howard). You cannot murder us all, and the survivors will testify to your misdeeds to destroy this boy's life and steal that plantation."

"That is true, I am here, and I am asserting my hereditary claim to Rokeby," said Howard.

At that moment Brackenridge drew his pistol and fired it directly at Howard's breast. His mark was true and accurate, but for the actions of Flora, who, after she screamed "NO!" lunged in front of Howard at the last moment, and the bullet meant for him struck the Sibyl squarely in the chest, killing her instantly. Brackenridge turned and fled down one of the many side tunnels that were present.

Hagenbach ordered the Yankee soldiers to shoot the rest, but before they could hardly proceed, there appeared a shadowy figure, of small but stout proportions, who in one motion knocked the weapons out of the hands of the soldiers, and proceeded to kill, in a most quick and summary fashion, both soldiers and Colonel Hagenbach by a swift and violent breaking of the neck, in an exhibition of tremendous strength.

Now the dark figure stepped into the light. Howard could see the form of what appeared to be a man, a Negro, of short height, but very developed upper body muscles, and large arms. He was dressed in very dirty and worn slave clothes, almost in the condition of rags. The rest of his appearance was equally singular, with hair that had never been shorn, and a long beard that had never been cut.

This could be only one person, thought Howard: The Wild Man of the Navidad!

Then Ben spoke up and said: "Flora always tole me dat de Wild Man weren't no monster or sperit at-all, dat he wuz human, an escaped slave, who had been a Prince in Africa. Dat he wuz too proud t' work in de fields, an so he preferred t' live as a wild animal."

The Wild Man, although supposedly not able to understand English, seemed to, by his expressions, agree with everything Ben was recounting about him.

By this time, Captain John Billups had grabbed George Brackenridge and returned him to the room where the gallows had been erected and had given him the choice of facing the Wild Man or signing over a Deed to Howard/Owen. Brackenridge opted to sign over the legal ownership to Howard/Owen of the entire plantation and surrounding ground at Rokeby, and accordingly, a paper and ink were procured from Hagenbach's office, and Brackenridge quickly drew up the deed, signed it, and delivered it to Richard Austin Howard, now Owens. Brackenridge was released, and he ran out the door, having evaded the fate of Hagenbach.

Howard gathered up the body of Flora gently and carried her out of the underground labyrinth beneath the Ruins. While they were climbing up out of the Ruins, they noticed that all the Yankee soldiers had fled for the safety of their warships that had been tied up along the river. Gunshots were then heard a little distance from the Ruins. A minute later, the party came upon William Stayton, walking toward the Ruins, and holding his smoking Sharps carbine rifle that he had never turned over to the Yankee Provost Marshal.

"Who have you got there?" said Stayton.

"Miss Flora. She is dead," said Howard/Owen.

"So is that Yankee lawyer-agent feller that I just ran into," said Stayton. "Brackenridge?"

"Yes, he saw me and for some reason, aimed his gun toward me, luckily ah had brought mah Sharp's carbine with me, and I beat him to the punch and dropped him dead. I reckon he is barkin' in Hell," said Stayton, fulfilling his promise of "killing all the Yankeys that lays in my power."

Chapter Thirty-Two

True Love is the gift which God has given
To man alone beneath the heaven,
It is not fantasy's hot fire,
Whose wishes, soon as granted, fly,
It liveth not in fierce desire,
With dead desire it doth not die,
It is the secret sympathy,
The silver link, the silken tie,
Which heart to heart, and mind to mind,
In body and in soul can bind.

— *Lay Of The Last Minstrel*, Canto V

Young Howard, now acknowledged as Clark Owen's son and heir, was restored to ownership of "Rokeby," when, after the death of Colonel Hagenbach, General Forbes and the rest of the Yankees fled their camp at the Ruins, and scrambled back to their gunboats in Carancahua Bay, and sailed away.

Local control of the county returned to the Confederates. The veterans of the Second Texas, the survivors, eventually made it back to Jackson County, some one-legged, some missing an arm, but all of them had a good story to tell those dear, wished-for future children and grandchildren: of the great Battle of Shiloh; of the gallant charge against Battery Robinett at Corinth; and of the trials and tribulations of the Siege of Vicksburg.

The locals never were able to convince the Wild Man to give up his solitary ways, although the country-folk were seldom visited by this mysterious man anymore after this incident. He mysteriously disappeared completely.

The tattered banner of the Second Texas was kept by Colonel Ashbel Smith, who entertained visitors to his study with the story of how it came to be smuggled out of Vicksburg, and of the young lady who accomplished that feat, "The Maid of Saragoza," Lucy Bertram.

Richard Austin Owen did not alter the manor house at Rokeby in any material way, except to restore it to the grand style it had enjoyed previously. He began to re-plant the gardens and grounds and stables destroyed by the hand of War and neglected by Brackenridge. Owen proposed marriage to Miss Bertram shortly after establishing himself at

"Rokeby," and instead of an engagement ring, gave her a locket inscribed with the Poet's words which form the motto to this Chapter.

Captain Billups, upon hearing of the happy news of the upcoming nuptials, stopped Owen on the street, and among the subjects which were discussed, were the couple's future, the future of Jackson County, and the likelihood of the Confederates ever actually achieving their long-sought for goal of Independence.

"Should the fortunes of war turn against us, and we not secure our Independence, I am sure Lucy and I shall become loyal citizens again," said Owen.

"Oh, I am certain Lucy will not, Richard! You know how she arises and excuses herself from the room, whenever Lincoln's name is mentioned! I think she is ready to fire one more cannon shot at the Yankees, Richard, if they dare to march up your front lawn!"

"Oh no, Captain, here endeth "*The Riven Oak and the Ivy*."

Notes

Note A. Wild Man of the Navidad.

This creature, or wild man, flourished in the Navidad river bottom areas of Jackson County for the better part of a decade, prior to the war. His story, or rather legend, has been so often written about and discussed, that it is difficult today to determine the facts from the romance. What is known is that this elusive, mysterious visitant would enter people's houses and take food, while apparently disdaining to take valuables lying in plain sight. While this is perhaps only indicative of natural hunger, other behavior was quite bizarre. The wild man would take several tools from a work shed, such as a handsaw, drawing knife and other tools useful to a woodworker, only to return them, several weeks later, to their original places, the handsaw scoured and polished as bright as silver (the polish that was put on the tools was wonderful skilled work. No one at this time knew that steel could be polished with such gloss, and no one knew the process by which it could be affected.)

It is known that guard dogs, otherwise faithful in their vigilance, were oblivious to the nighttime forays of the wild man. The negroes were absolutely terrified of him and referred to him simply as IT or THAT THING THAT COMES.

Despite many concerted efforts to trap or capture the wild man, he always eluded his would-be captors. Once, or twice, his pursuers found his 'home' or 'hideout' in a canebrake along the river bottoms, and various items taken out of homes were recognized. However, the quarry itself, the wild man, was never 'home' at the time.

When the wild man's reign of terror ended, it was none too clear about what the reason for its termination had been, or what eventually became of him. He may, or may not, have ended up as portrayed in the romance.

Note B. Karankawa Indians.

"Karankawa" was an old Indian name meaning "The Water Walkers," and the indigenous tribe of Indians that the first settlers of Jackson County encountered were so called because of their habit of wading in water to catch their food: oysters, clams, shrimps, crabs and fish, along the salt marshes and shallow water in the bays. The Karankawa were noted for cannibalism, for being giants in stature, and for having ugly faces rendered hideous by alligator grease and dirt with which they were besmeared from head to foot, as a defense against mosquitoes. The French found that they neither kept time either by the sun nor the moon, and that they were a seacoast tribe, low in training and mentality. The French colony established by LaSalle, was massacred by the Karankawa. Unable to be Christianized or civilized, they were exterminated, having given their name to some of our bodies of water, and their burial mounds are all that remain of this race of giant cannibalistic Indians.

Note C. Whistling Dick.

Students of the Siege of Vicksburg will of course smile at the reference to Whistling Dick's shells being "two hundred pounds." Whistling Dick was, in fact, an older model 18-pounder smoothbore that had been rifled by the Confederates and, for all the reasons mentioned in the text, made such a vivid impression on the Yankees, with its sound and its accuracy, that the Yankees, in effect, embellished some of "Dick's" accomplishments and attributes, and it led their imagination running wild to some extent. However, there is no doubt "Dick" figured substantially in the sinking of the *Cincinnati*, as stated in the text. Interestingly, there is speculation that one of the two English Whitworth rifled cannons in the Vicksburg defenses, and which had a similar whistling sound when fired, was at times, confused with Whistling Dick.

Note D. Sterling Fisher.

Those familiar with the Second Texas may already know that the remarkable story of Sterling Fisher, and the Yankee he helped on the Shiloh battlefield, is entirely true, and that Fisher indeed survived the war thanks to his Yankee friend, and lived on until 1908.

7UP

The End

The Riven Oak and the Ivy

~ OR ~

The Maid of Saragoza

or The Maid of Saragoza

www.ingramcontent.com/pod-product-compliance
Lightning Source LLC
Chambersburg PA
CBHW050320120526
44592CB00014B/1984